THE ONLY
"LIKE"
THAT MATTERS IS
GOD'S

THE ONLY
"LIKE"
THAT MATTERS IS
GOD'S

Using the Bible to Transform
Your Life on Social Media

TERYN GREGSON

Good Books® books may be purchased in bulk at special discounts for sales promotion, corporate gifts, fund-raising, or educational purposes. Special editions can also be created to specifications. For details, contact the Special Sales Department, Good Books, 307 West 36th Street, 11th Floor, New York, NY 10018 or info@skyhorsepublishing.com.

Good Books is an imprint of Skyhorse Publishing, Inc.®, a Delaware corporation. Visit our website at www.goodbooks.com.

10 9 8 7 6 5 4 3 2 1

Library of Congress Cataloging-in-Publication Data is available on file.

Print ISBN: 978-1-68099-914-3
Ebook ISBN: 978-1-68099-931-0

Cover photograph by Getty Images

Printed in the United States of America

Author's Note & Prayer

The Holy Spirit prompted me to write this book back in 2020, when my life was a picture-perfect Instagram profile online. My career was soaring, my husband and I had just welcomed our first child into the world, and everything seemed absolutely perfect, especially to those scrolling through my social media feed.

However, it all came crashing down in November 2021, when I lost my sports media career, resulting in public backlash. I also lost my book agent and all prospects of this writing finding the shelves.

God always has a plan, especially if you remain faithful to Him through your highs and lows. The trials I've endured since, including being canceled online, have added to this book in ways that I pray will help you through any sacrifice or online struggle you may be having.

God's timing is perfect. So, I know this is finding your hands exactly at the time He ordained.

And you show that you are a letter from Christ delivered by us, written
not with ink but with the Spirit of the Living God, not on tablets of
stone but on tablets of human hearts.
—2 Corinthians 3:3

Each time I sat down to write, I prayed that God would give me the words He wanted me to share with others and a miraculous thing happened. He would point me to topics and verses that shaped this book. It is, therefore, written and guided by the Spirit of the Living God; I owe all the glory to Him.

I pray that His message will be written, not just in this book but on your heart, and that you will share His message with others. So that we can escape the shackles of social media and turn to Christ to set us free.

Amen.

Devotional Note

Whether you are going through this book on your own, or as a small group, class, or book club, I pray that you will take the time to dig deeper, open your Bible and answer the devotional questions provided at the end of each chapter.

Get out your pen, mark it up, and don't be afraid to highlight or make notes in your book and devotionals. A few years later, you'll love seeing what really hit home for you when you originally went through this text.

A good book is well loved. And studied scripture is well marked.

God bless!

Table of Contents

Introduction

Do you feel that tug? That urge to pick up your phone and browse? Like you have a few minutes to spare and can't help but pass that time on your device? Maybe you'd rather spend that time present, in the moment, taking in the world around you. But . . . You. Just. Can't. Help. It.

Social media feels like it has taken over. From dating to our careers, it is so ingrained in how we operate. It feels impossible to avoid using, even if we wanted to give it up altogether. We have to be meticulously intentional or exert extra effort to use more traditional means of communication or information consumption instead of social media in most areas of our lives:

- People utilize apps to meet their prospective partners. I can't say that I have ever used a dating site, but I've definitely scrubbed ex-boyfriends from my social media profiles.
- Anybody else refresh their page multiple times to see how many likes their recent post received? Or is that just me?
- Is your device the main or only place you get the news and information you need?

- Have you gone from reading books you can hold in your hand to just consuming the scroll?
- Does looking through the comments section make your blood boil?
- Or maybe you are like me, and your entire career is now online!

Have you begun to wonder how we got here? How did we get ourselves to the point where social media, news, or whatever else we consume on our phones seems to draw us in without even thinking about it? Like it's beyond our control? We're all facing a similar struggle, to strike a healthy balance between being the consumer and being consumed. We suspect that what the world out there is consuming isn't filling us up, that there's a missing piece.

Do you feel something else quietly calling you?

Countless times in history, God has allowed His people to stray from Him, only for them to realize they need Him more than ever. God uses everything for His purposes and, I believe, He's actually using social media to bring us closer to Him. Social media has left us empty, but He's using it for good—to bring us closer to the Truth and to help others see it, too.

If you feel that struggle inside, that means you're closer to the Holy Spirit than you think. You are likely feeling all these things because you sense there's a difference between the way the world uses social media and the way you would like to. You feel that tug because God is calling you down a different path. His Son tells us repeatedly throughout the Gospels that Christians are called to be different from the world. He's tugging at our hearts right now, telling us to use and consume online content in a different way than the rest of the world does. And for social media to be the catalyst that allows us to realize we are longing to get back to a closer relationship with Him.

The age of social media may be young, but the obstacles it presents to us are nothing new under the sun. TikTok, Twitter, YouTube, Instagram, and other social media platforms may have been invented nearly two thousand years after Christ was born, but the Bible is still our handbook for how to participate in, consume, and combat this uncharted era of social media. Influencers are not new. Comparison and boasting are not new. The promotion of false ideas and idols is not new.

Mankind has faced all of these issues in various forms, since Eve ate from the tree of knowledge of good and evil. Therefore, nothing is new to God, and nothing is a surprise to Him. His Word is complete and sufficient. Social media might not be mentioned specifically in His text, but that doesn't stop the Living Word from telling us exactly how to use it. We, as people, made in His image, have been following social influencers for centuries! And, without a doubt, the most important "follow" of our lives is Christ. Move over, Kim Kardashian; Jesus Christ has way more followers throughout history than you and your entire family combined!

Even better news, Jesus doesn't care who or how many follow you, he only cares that you follow him!

So I pray this book takes the pressure off of you to collect a certain number of followers; that it allows you to let go of the anxiety that comes from comparing yourself to what you see in other people's Instagram feeds; that it takes away your desire to get countless "likes" on your post; that it gives you the tools to limit your time scrolling on your device and that it instead moves you to glorify Him. With Christ, you have the power to escape the tempting influence of society. Instead, you can turn your attention to influencing others for eternity. You can glorify God through how you present yourself, consume, and operate on social media, regardless of your social media status.

Because the only "like" that matters, is God's.

> "For the eyes of the Lord roam throughout the earth, so that He may strongly support those whose heart is completely His."
> —2 Chronicles 16:9 NASB

CHAPTER 1

The Simultaneous Birth
of Social Media and My Career

Take a moment and think of a time before social media. What was life like? How old were you? What sort of troubles did you have? Was it a more joyful time? Now fast forward in your memory to when you created your first social media account. What platform did you choose? Why? What troubles or worries came after? What highs and lows did you experience because of it? Do you like your life better before or after it? Regardless of how you answer that last question, the reality is social media is here to stay for the foreseeable future. You can't control that, but you can control how you use, consume, or to what extent you take part in it.

I came into social media kicking and screaming in 2007. Facebook, which had been created a few years prior in 2004, began picking up steam at that point, while I was in high school. At the time, because of how new it was, I had no interest in getting involved. But my friends refused to let me go away to college without it, so I gave in and made a profile. They swore it was the only way we'd stay in touch.

"What are phones for?" I said.

Receiving my own cell phone as I went away to college felt like an accomplishment in and of itself. Prior, I had to borrow my mom's phone anytime I left the house. Phones, at this point, were not engrained in a teen's rite of passage yet. My phone plan didn't even have text messaging. (Again, what are phones for?! If you want to talk to me, call me!) Fast forward to my sophomore year at the University of Missouri Journalism School. A lot had changed. I had given in to peer pressure, yet again, and gotten unlimited text messaging for my cell phone. I had hundreds of photos and Facebook posts to my name. I lived in an apartment off campus, and I started working at the local NBC television station as a producer, photographer, and reporter at the age of nineteen. I thought I was dominating!

So, when my professor and news director came into the newsroom, and declared all reporters were required to get Twitter, I bet you can guess what my reaction was. (Remember, I was dominating life at this point, I thought I knew it all!)

"There's no way," I said. "Why do I need Twitter? All anyone does on Twitter is tell people about what they had for lunch."

"Going to the grocery store today."

"Just saw a movie!"

"I haven't washed my hair in three days."

You're either laughing because you remember the ripe young days of social media, or you were not out of diapers yet and this sounds ridiculous. But this is what people were tweeting about when Twitter first came out. No one knew how to use it back then, and I would argue many still don't today.

I'll never forget what the news director said to the entire group of objecting young reporters.

"You are going to be tweeting about something far more important. You are going to be tweeting about the news."

It was like the studio lights were pointing on him and he was Ron Burgundy himself.

"You are going to be tweeting about THE NEWS!"

Genius! Why hadn't I thought of that?

I also never thought social media would become my career either. The advent of Twitter and my first news director's forethought to utilize it for news, you could say, was perfect timing. I graduated with a degree in journalism and entered "the real world" armed with my limited knowledge of social media. Turns out, that limited knowledge was far more than most companies had. Deep down, I had this feeling that the media industry was about to drastically change, and I wanted to be a part of it. Finding a job in media after college took several years of networking, but eventually, I landed at the St. Louis Cardinals as their first in-house digital reporter. It was a dream that kick-started my career in mainstream social media. In-house content creation was a revolutionary concept at the time. In 2014, news outlets were still the content kings. Newspapers, radio and television stations, and a few independent websites were the main outlets creating content. The industry changed quickly. Everyone jumped on the bandwagon and in just a matter of a few years, it became the industry norm for organizations to have their own content and social media teams. My career changed just as quickly, too. I went from the St. Louis Cardinals to CBSSports.com to PGA TOUR media in less than two years. The industry was changing so fast, we could all hardly keep up!

Why am I taking you down my career path? Because social media can be what you do, but doesn't have to overcome you. You can go so far as to make it your career, while at the same time, remain true to your belief system, true to your morals, true to Him. Or it can simply be what you look at and consume, without changing what you believe. It can be a force for good, despite the bad. It won't be easy, it won't be popular, and it won't make you Instagram famous.

It doesn't matter how many "likes" you get. Only one "like" matters.

God's.

And He can set you free from society's social media shackles.

Chapter 1 Devotional

1. Take a moment and think of a time before social media.

   • What was life like?

   • How old were you?

   • What sort of troubles did you have?

   • Was it a more joyful time?

2. Now fast forward in your memory to when you created your first social media account.

- What platform did you choose?

- Why?

- What troubles or worries came after?

- What highs and lows did you experience because of it?

- Do you like your life better before or after it?

3. Do you consume social media? Or are you consumed by it?

4. Are your thoughts or beliefs sometimes shaped by what you see on social media? Give an example.

5. Do you wonder what people will think of your post before you publish it?

6. Do you ever wonder what God would think of your post before you publish it?

7. Would putting His approval first change any of the posts you've published?

8. Would putting His approval first, over what accounts you follow, or what you allow to influence you, make a difference in your social media life"? (Are there any accounts you'd unfollow?)

9. Ask God for forgiveness from your social media habits. Freeing yourself by knowing that as you seek His approval, you don't actually earn it. He's given His favor as a gift to you through the blood of His Son. Using what pleases Him as your guide, is what will have the greatest positive impact on your social media life.

Prayer

Dear Lord,

Your amazing relationship with me is beyond my scope of understanding but I am so blessed you have brought me here. Thank you for working to draw me closer to You by analyzing my social media habits, follows, and consumption. Help me to frame my approach to content through a Biblical worldview. And equip me to impact others through the adjustments I make to the time, people, and channels I consume on my devices. Allow the time spent in this book and its devotionals to open the door to having an eternal impact.

Amen.

CHAPTER 2
Faith Filter

You call yourself a Christian, but you follow celebrities on social media that post provocative photos or promote non-Christian lifestyles. Perhaps you read, or maybe even post your own, malicious comments because the content you consume sparks hatred, envy, or jealousy. All of these embody the works of the flesh, the Apostle Paul outlines, as opposites to the fruit of the Spirit in Galatians 5. Paul warns that those who take part in things like sexual immorality, moral impurity, promiscuity, idolatry, witchcraft, hatreds, strife, jealousy, outbursts of anger, selfish ambitions, dissensions, divisions, envy, and more will not inherit the kingdom of God [Galatians 5:19-21]. Though jarring when read aloud, the works of the flesh are easy to fall into online, usually subtly escalating over time.

While this experience is true for many, perhaps your social media troubles are seemingly more innocent. Maybe you spend more time on social media than time face-to-face with your family, friends, or neighbors, despite the Bible's call to fellowship both for your sake and for others. Or maybe you are like many around you who have allowed social media to become your source of truth, letting others shape and decide what you think. Many of us, myself included at times, have become more familiar with what's being fed to us online than the content in our bibles.

Give yourself grace. It's been a process for all of us.

Social media came, evolved, and has impacted our world so quickly. It's only natural that it takes us time to figure out how to use it— likely a lot more time than it did for social media to take over the globe. Social media is a secular billboard. Depending on who you follow, you are likely doused in secular ideas left and right as you scroll. The majority of those ideas are not biblically rooted. Some of the most deceptive messaging seems good on the surface but as you peel back the layers, you will find that it's not. The more we consume of worldly ideology, the less we are taking in God's biblical truths.

The Psalmist in Psalm 1 speaks of a righteous person, one who is not walking in the ways of the world.

> "How happy is the one who does not walk in the advice of the wicked
> or stand in the pathway with sinners or sit in the company of mockers!"
> —Psalm 1:1

It may seem harsh, but the wicked are those who are not believers. Yes, we are all sinners, but those who walk in, don't turn away from, and even delight in their sin—or mock the Bible with their unbelief—are those of the secular world the Psalmist is speaking. The ESV Study Bible puts it well, "The truly happy person guides his life by God's instruction rather than by the advice of those who reject that instruction." But how do you know if you are walking in the way of the Lord and not the way of the world? The Psalmist tells us, your "delight is in the Lord's instruction, and he meditates on it day and night." [Psalm 1:2] Do you seek out the Word? Do you hunger for the fruit of God's knowledge? Then you are walking in the ways of the Lord our God and are not entranced by the world.

Social media can easily pull us into that worldly trance and distract us from picking up our bibles and, instead, sucks us into our newsfeeds.

That's why we as Christians need boundaries. We need to pay attention to who and what we follow, and we need our own filter. Just like you see influencers using custom filters or the makeup filter on Instagram and TikTok to make themselves look flawless, or your friends use the silly face filter for fun, we have our own filter and it's richer, brighter, and more fulfilling than anything Big Tech could ever present us. God tells us to use His filter. Filter everything you do, even what you do on social media, through Him—through a *Faith Filter*.

"So, whether you eat or drink, or whatever you do,
do all to the glory of God."
—1 Corinthians10:31 ESV

Many of us consume social media just as much, or even more, than we eat or drink, don't we? Are you using social media for His glory? For every piece of content we consume, we should be asking ourselves, "is this biblical?" The Faith Filter is how you see the world, it shapes your worldview. It is the lens through which you take in every piece of content or information that you come across. Do you embrace it as biblically true, dismiss it as biblically inaccurate, or investigate it because you are unsure of how it measures up to scripture? It can also influence your behaviors and attitude and can move you to glorify God in most every area of your life.

Over time, using our Faith Filters online will become second nature. The more you practice applying your biblical worldview to your social media consumption, the more it will become engrained in you. Start by using your Faith Filter on social media and it could translate into every part of your life. Social media could actually turn out to be a blessing if the Faith Filter principle is used for spreading God's glory and adopted more broadly among people.

Even as someone who has been there since the birth of social media and grown as a young adult with it in my life, the road hasn't been easy for me, either. Though so much of my career has required me to know the ins and outs of social media, I haven't always known how to navigate it personally and am still learning and trying to get better with it every day. I'm also getting braver, and I see others are, too. Even though I've known God my entire life, it wasn't until the last few years of my sports media career that I became outspoken about my faith online. I received hateful comments, lost followers, and I even lost my dream job following my faith. But I found myself. Or better yet, I found myself in Christ. And an entire new community of believers who have strengthened my faith.

Jesus tells us that the path to follow him will be difficult and that we will face persecution [John 15:20]. But he also tells us that his yoke is easy and his burden is light. [Matthew 11:30]. Traditionally, a yoke was shared between a pair of oxen to pull a wagon or load. Jesus takes up the second yoke alongside you and makes the loads of life lighter for you.

> "Take my yoke upon you, and learn from me, for I am gentle and lowly in heart and you will find rest for your souls."
> Matthew 11:29

When using the Faith Filter, you will be stepping out of the mainstream. Embrace it! Because you will be stepping into Jesus's open arms, where you will find peace, strength, and wisdom. We must look to him as our model for righteous behavior and his Father's favor is the only one we should seek. His "like" is all we need. We don't deserve it; we can't earn it. He gives us all His "likes" for free.

> "For by grace you have been saved through faith.
> And this is not your own doing; it is the gift of God,
> not a result of works, so that no one may boast."
> —Ephesians 2:8-9

We have been chosen by a gracious God—one who has guided us through scripture to filter our lives through the lens of our faith. He wants us to consider Him in every aspect of our lives because He enriches our lives. As the bible states, we have a jealous God. Not jealous in the way that one might be jealous of a social media star, i.e., jealous of their fame and free stuff. That is a self-centered view of jealousy, meanwhile God is always considering all of us. The Hebrew word *qana* is used in the Old Testament, which suggests a deep and intense emotion that can be negative or, in this case, positive, like in the boundless love God feels for His people.[1] God is jealous, or—more easily comprehended by our modern minds—impassioned, "for our own good, that we may share His holiness." [Hebrews 12:10] This is one way God has been urging us to use the Faith Filter since the Old Testament.

"Do not bow in worship to them, and do not serve them;
for I, the Lord your God, am a jealous God, bringing the consequences
of the father's iniquity on the children to the third and
fourth generations of those who hate me."
—Exodus 20:5 ESV

God is intensely interested in where our hearts reside because He doesn't want us to worship other gods. Not for His selfish desires; he doesn't *need* to be worshiped by anyone. He's actually protecting us. This "jealousy" is for our benefit. He doesn't want us to serve other gods or make other idols because it will only lead us to destruction. His Word gives us warnings of entire kingdoms falling because they turn away from God and allow their lives to be ruled by idols constructed by man. Paul sounds the alarm against idolatry in the works of the flesh, urging us to turn away from following such things so we can inherit the kingdom of God. Our Creator, at the throne of the kingdom cares for us. He doesn't want to see us led astray, just like a caring father doesn't want to see his child go down the wrong path. If we do venture down the path the world would like us to, our destruction could not only have consequences on our own souls, but could have a negative effect for generations to come. Aren't we already seeing the consequences of social media? It is our responsibility, as the first generation of social media users, to stop ourselves from giving in and worshiping this unworthy idol. If we don't? The third and fourth generations after us could suffer the consequences. As humans we are easily distracted by idols, big or small, in our lives. It doesn't take long for people to forget about God and all He's done for us.

The Bible warns us that the awe-inspiring fear, respect, and adoration of the Lord can be lost in a short period of time. We can heed its warnings and learn from our ancestors. The first generation of God's chosen people to inhabit the Promised Land can be a lesson for us all. Their comfortable life of ease and distraction took them away from the God who had rescued their grandparents. They were slaves, who leaned on God in the unimaginable times of their servitude, but easily forgot about filtering their needs through their faith in the Lord overtime.

> "When all that generation had been gathered to their fathers, another generation arose after them who did not know the Lord nor the work which He had done for Israel. Then the children of Israel . . . forsook the Lord God of their fathers, who had brought them out of the land of Egypt; and they followed other gods from among the gods of the people who were all around them."
> —Judges 2:10–12

Moses led God's people, as Egyptian slaves, out of Egypt. Those slaves groaned and complained to God on their journey to the Promised Land, even though God was saving them! Due to their lapse in faith, God punished them and Moses to wander the wilderness for forty years and then allowed Joshua and the next generation after them to enter the land He set aside for His people. The second generation—the children of Moses's time—saw what wrath awaited them if they did not follow God, as they knew first-hand of their parent's punishment. Yet, the grandchildren of the slaves forgot about the enslaved suffering their forefathers endured. They were ungrateful of the privilege of being the first to live their entire lives in the Promised Land. In their comfort, they quickly allowed other idols to form in their lives. They moved on to worship other gods. It only took one generation to forget!

We are the first generation of social media users. Will we or our children soon forget, too? Have we already forgotten? Or can social media be our wake-up call to show us our need to lean on God? What came next for God's people who cast Him aside in the Promised Land was approximately three hundred years of appointed judges like Deborah, Gideon, etc. who were temporary leaders, followed by their cries for an earthly king.

Everything written in the Bible is breathed out by God. Every word, every verse, every chapter is important. But it's especially important when something is repeated; it means God wants you to pay close attention to what He's telling you. Repetition is God's emphasis in the Bible. The story of His people begging for an earthly king and going through cycle after cycle of idol-worshipping men ruling over them is repeated not just once, but twice in the Bible. Just like the Gospels are four different accounts of Jesus's ministry on earth, 1 & 2 Kings and 1 & 2 Chronicles are the telling of the same story from different perspectives. Thirty-seven generations of Israel's kings, starting with Saul and David, and continuing all the way through until the final reign with King Josiah worshipped false gods for four and a half centuries. The kings after David and his son Solomon did as God commanded them not to do and married and intermingled with the pagan populations that worshiped numerous other gods in hopes of bringing them rain, wealth, crops, fertility, you name it.

From about 970 BC to 560 BC the people commonly worshiped multiple gods by building what they called "high places"—temples or altars set up on a hill, mountaintop, or the highest place in a city. The high places served as a place of worship to light incense and bring an offering to a particular god they were asking something of. Some of these temples were home to prostitutes and promoted other debaucheries in the name of pagan worship.

Of course, these Jewish kings knew that they only had one true God, but for some reason many of them let those high places remain. Some Jewish kings also participated in worship or asked these man-made gods for food, rain, wealth, or other ways to fulfill their materialistic needs. Generation-after-generation, reign-after-reign, God commanded each king to tear down the high places. Most of them would say something along the lines of, "Yeah, God, you got it. Consider it done." Then time would pass, wars would happen, or they'd marry a pagan woman who worshiped the false idols.

"Yet the high places were not taken away," something always got in the way. This exact same language is used numerous times in the Old Testament. [1 Kings 15:14, 1 Kings 22:43, 2 Kings 12:3, 2 Kings 14:4, 2 Kings 15:4, 2 Kings 15:35, 2 Chronicles 15:17, 2 Chronicles 20:33] God, the faithful Father, told his children the same thing, repeatedly, but they always made an excuse for the high places to remain. Yet, He remained patient.

Jehoshaphat and Jotham were two of the few kings that truly loved the Lord and asked their people to turn their hearts to God, but they did not tear down the high places. Therefore, the cycle continued after they left power. Hezekiah was the one king who finally tore down the high places. Hezekiah loved the Lord and enacted a religious revival unmatched by all the other kings. His love and trust in the Lord led him to defeat the powerful Assyrians. Later in life, Hezekiah had a different idol. He showed off his wealth adorned inside the Lord's temple to the Babylonians, Israel's enemy, and they came back and ransacked him later. Many today can relate to Hezekiah, idolizing their own wealth or dreaming of obtaining the wealth seen on others' social media feeds. If we don't conquer our idols, they can affect those that come after us. For example, Hezekiah's son and heir Manasseh was the most evil king to rule in Judah. Talk about forgetting God in just one generation!

Two generations later, King Josiah reigned. He was the last good king and the final king before Israel's Babylonian captivity. While Josiah was rebuilding Hezekiah's temple that the previous two kings abandoned, he discovered a mysterious book. The book—not mysterious to us today—was the first parts of the Bible! And it had been lost and forgotten in just a few lifetimes. Josiah, in awe of the truth within this rediscovered book, took swift action to return his kingdom to faith and remove pagan worship. But after he died, the final two kings of Judah forgot about the Lord and eventually the Babylonians finally brought about the destruction of Judah. Babylonian King Nebuchadnezzar is infamous in history for building his lavish kingdoms and conquering anyone who stood in his way. Babylon worshipped its pagan gods until the Persians conquered them.

Have we let social media conquer us? Have we made it our high place? Is it something we put on a pedestal? It is important we know and understand our Christian history so we can glean wisdom from the mistakes that have been made by those that have come before us, those that have neglected to fully filter their lives through their faith.

You likely don't worship social media intentionally or view it as something sacred. But the definition of "idolize" is "to love and admire to excess." Do you use social media to excess? Do you allow it to consume your day? Do you open up Facebook or Instagram whenever you get an alert on your phone and then realize later that you've just wasted twenty minutes, thirty minutes, or maybe even an hour of your time unintentionally on your device?

> "I do not understand what I am doing, because I do not practice what I want to do, but I do what I hate . . . for I do not do the good that I want to do, but practice the evil that I do not want to do."
> —Romans 7:15, 19 ESV

The Old Testament Jewish kings didn't consider those pagan gods to be their idols either, yet they let them remain. They still occasionally went up to the high places and worshiped, while, at the same time, claiming to love the one true God. We worship what we spend our time on—intentionally or unintentionally.

Samuel was the first of the kings' prophets, who served as an advisor to King Saul and King David. He warned the people about diverting their time from God to things of little worth, in the frame of eternity.

> "Samuel replied, 'Don't be afraid. Even though you have committed all this evil, don't turn away from following the Lord. Instead, worship the Lord with all your heart. Don't turn away to follow worthless things that can't profit or rescue you; they are worthless.'"
> —1 Samuel 12:20-21 CSB

So, what's the answer? Delete social media and stay off of it altogether? Maybe. Or you could turn to the Holy Spirit to remove it as an idol in your life and no longer let it be a high place, but a tool you look at differently, one where you use the "Faith Filter" to navigate at all times. Make a conscious decision about how much time you spend on social media and what type of content you are consuming. Use it as one of many great sources to spread the gospel, connect with other Christians, and let His light shine for others to see; not as a *replacement* for your time reading the Bible or your in-person fellowship because you consume photos of verses on Instagram instead, or joined a Facebook chat instead of a bible study group, or watch sermons online. Online enhancements to worship are a wonderful booster to your time with the Lord, but the Bible still urges us to pick it up, read it in context, and be there with one another in Christian fellowship.

Make social media a tool, not an idol.

It's never too late to ask God to search your heart, help lead you down the right path, or remove any unworthy idols in your life. Because God will never leave you. He always keeps His promises. After the vicious cycle of kings led to a hostile takeover, the Jews were exiled to Babylon and Persia. Yet, God kept His promise to His people that He shared through Jeremiah's prophecy [Jeremiah 25:12, 32: 36–38] and delivered them from foreign exile.

> "I have banished them in my anger, rage, and intense wrath, and I will return them to this place and make them live in safety. They will be my people and I will be their God."
> —Jeremiah 32:38

God used Ezra and Nehemiah to take His people back home to Jerusalem and rebuild the city walls and the temple. All of that led to Jesus a few hundred years later, when God would send His only Son to remove the need for a temple building. Now Christ dwells within us. Nothing can separate us from His love: Not appointed leaders, not our modern struggles. No matter what, Jesus is always with us. However, we cannot connect with the Holy Spirit living within us if we drown it out with the noise and distraction of our devices.

But perhaps social media can be the catalyst for us realizing that the fast-pace, busy structure of our modern lives is keeping us from an intimate relationship with Christ. We've been on this path for a while, each generation making their lives more and more full of the newest activities, technologies, and distractions. Social media could be the lens that exposes how all these things are damaging our children and society, forcing us to reevaluate, slow down, and lean into our faith.

Despite Israel repeatedly straying in their faith, God remained faithful and was merciful. That was true then in 444 BC and is true today. Our devices have become the center of our existence. And because our phones are always in our hands, we think our lives are, too. But we have to find peace in trust. God loves us and gave us free will, but ultimately we can trust our lives to Him and become at peace with our inability to control *everything*. We become more attuned to God's glorious sovereignty when we become cognizant of our surroundings, by putting down our phones and opening our eyes to the beauty of God's creation: listening to the birds chirping and children laughing, seeing the flowers blooming and the sky glowing. We didn't make any of that, God did. And He ordained us to be stewards of His Creation, but our devices distract us from doing so.

If our almighty Creator can make all the beauties of this world and the unimaginable glory of the heavens that await us, He can sculpt our lives in magnificent ways. He has a grand plan, one specifically designed for each of us. The sooner we realize the Creator of the Universe is out for our best interest, the sooner we are able to make room for Him to do His will. But that also involves relinquishing control and crossing over into authentic trust. We must strike a balance of putting complete trust in God's glorious sovereignty and our call to exercise our faith, through pouring ourselves into our faith journey. We can do so by having faith that God will provide, despite sometimes being called to work our way down a path different than society glorifies. God defines faith in Hebrews 11:1 "as the assurance of things hoped for, the conviction of things not seen." And goes on to explain:

"By faith we understand the universe was created by the word of God,
so that what is seen was not made out of what is visible."
—Hebrews 11:3

We are encouraged to take the leap of applying the Faith Filter to our lives when we look at real examples of people who have let faith guide their discernment, actions, and decisions listed out in *the Hall of Faith* outlined in the verses that follow Hebrews 11:3. *The Hall of Faith*, as it has become known, is a summary of many of the people in the Bible that accomplished great things for God's Kingdom through their faith. They were not perfect and their individual journeys of working on and using their Faith Filter were also far from perfect, but God still used them in extraordinary ways to carry out His great plan through their faith. Those listed include familiar Biblical figures, some of which we'll look at in this book and chapter devotionals, including Abel, Enoch, Noah, Abraham, Sarah, Isaac, Jacob, Joseph, Moses, Rahab, Gideon, Barak, Samson, Jephthah, David, Samuel, and the prophets. The Bible goes on to encourage us to "run the race with endurance" like these *Hall of Faith* members, by "looking to Jesus as the founder and perfecter of our faith." [Hebrews 12:1–2] And we can turn to Him as the source of our faith because he "endured the cross, despising the shame and is seated at the right hand of the throne of God."

So how do we give "the founder and perfecter of our faith" sovereignty over the "Faith Filter" in our lives? Missionary Elisabeth Elliot, in her book *Keep a Quiet Heart,*[2] poignantly explains ways we *do not* let faith work in our lives. Instead, so many of us let worry consume us [Philippians 4:6], refuse to accept what God gives [Matthew 11:29], try to rule our own lives [Colossians 3:15], or carry all of our burdens by ourselves [1 Peter 5:7], so we look for peace in places like social media instead of God [John 14:27].

Bury yourself in your bible instead of your social media feed to look up those corresponding verses in order to choose peace in the Lord. If you are in a phase in your life where everything is spiraling out of control and nothing seems to be in your control, choose to go to God—rather than modern distractions that claim they will help you, but in the end, don't have a lasting hold. When you start to go to God for everything, even the little things, an amazing thing can happen: An inner dialogue with God bursts open. You don't just talk to Him about the hard things, you talk to Him all day long about anything.

> "Lord, help me meet my struggles today."
> "Father, my baby is crying, please comfort her."
> "Glorious Creator, how beautiful is this sunny day?!"
> "Gracious God, I am so grateful for my husband's smile."
> Or simply, "thank you Lord." For just about anything that makes your heart swell.

Jesus brought joy to his faith in the perfect manner and is the one we should look to help us anytime we are struggling with trusting God. Hebrews 12:2 also states that "Jesus, the founder and perfecter of our faith, who for the joy set before him, endured the cross." Jesus, putting all his faith in God, went to the cross knowing what suffering was awaiting him with *joy*. Our Savior made the ultimate act of faith gladly. His joy that stems from his unwavering faith in God can inspire us to use the Faith Filter, despite the things in our lives that try to hold us back. Whether it's big hurdles in our lives or common struggles on social media, like comparison and losing sight of the gratitude Jesus had, these challenges are essential for us to examine and work to overcome. As we overcome them, with the help of tools like discernment and rest, we can be grateful to God and our Faith Filter will shine through.

Chapter 2 Devotional

1. Are there any ways that your current social media habits allow some of the works of the flesh that Paul outlines in Galatians 5:19–21 to creep into your life?

   • List each work of the flesh that applies to you and how.

2. In Psalm 1:1, the psalmist warns us not to model our lives after non-believers. Do you look up to anyone on social media that embodies more of the works of the flesh, instead of the fruits of the Spirit? Who?

   • Should you filter those accounts through your Faith Filter instead? How?

3. According to the end of that Psalm in verse 1:6, will the ways of the Lord last for eternity or will the ways of those who do not live by faith?

- Does realizing that God's Word urges us to filter in those that live by faith and be cautious of those that do not prompt you to want to make any changes to who you follow on social media? Outline who and why below.

4. What are other ways you can apply the Faith Filter to how you use your devices?

5. There are many ways we resist using the Faith Filter and *do not* let the peace of God's sovereignty work in our lives. Circle which of the following you identify with. Look up the corresponding passage.

- Resent God's ways. [Psalm 119:165]
- Worry consumes you. [Philippians 4:6]
- Pray only about things you
    can't control by yourself. [Philippians 4:6, 7]
- Refuse to accept God's will. [Matthew 11:29]
- Look for peace elsewhere than in Him. [John 14:27]
- Try to rule your own life. [Colossians 3:15]
- Doubt God's Word. [Romans 15:13]
- Carry all your burdens. [1 Peter 5:7]

6. In what ways have you made social media an idol in your life?

FAITH FILTER CHALLENGE

7. It only took one generation for the Israelites to forget about God. Let's take a look at how recent history has shaped *your* generation's heart posture toward the Lord. Keeping in mind our biblical example of Moses's generation, who were slaves, versus their grandchildren, who were the first to live their entire lives in the Promised Land: what *world* circumstances/struggles did your grandparents endure?

   • If you are a grandparent, parent, or soon-to-be parent. (Examples: Great Depression, World War II)

   • If you are a teen or young adult: (Example: Prosperous US Economy of the Eighties and Nineties)

8. Looking back at past examples from history can help us put our own times into perspective. Keeping in mind our biblical example of Moses's grandchildren, who forgot about the hardships their grandparents endured: what *world* circumstances have you grown up in?

   A. If you are a grandparent, parent, or soon-to-be parent:

   • Have you forgotten the hardships your grandparents went through?

- Do you feel like your generation has left the church or turned from the Word and teachings of God?

- Do you take into consideration the legacy of social media you are leaving behind for the next generation? How do you think it has or will impact them?

B. If you are a teen or young adult:

- Do you feel like it is a tougher or easier time to grow up than your parents or grandparents?

- Do you feel like your generation is searching for a more solid foundation than what social media has set you up with?

- Do you feel like some are starting to find that foundation in the Lord?

9. After looking at your grandparents' circumstances, versus your generation's circumstances, how do you assess your generation's heart posture toward the Lord? Has your generation forgotten about God? Or is it searching to return back to God as its foundation?

Prayer

Dear Lord,

You are the One and Only that we should be filtering everything through. Please help me to focus my eyes on you, not on my social media scroll. Please forgive all the times I've wasted on social media and help me turn away from this idol, big or small, in my life. Now, as I look to the future, reroute my habits. Allow me to use social media as a tool to glorify your kingdom. Help me to go through the steps of using your Faith Filter when I consume or post on social media. Guide me to understand what that Faith Filter looks like for Your will to be done. Thank you for your everlasting grace and forgiveness.

Amen.

Chapter 3

Comparison

After I graduated from college, with a broadcast journalism degree in hand, I moved back home with my parents. No job, no prospects. The market had just crashed, and news stations were cutting spending and laying off staff. The odds were not in my favor. I spent my days calling and emailing news stations, radio stations, and sports teams trying to get someone to have coffee with me. Many kind people took me up on that cup of coffee and were gracious enough to talk to me, but they simply didn't have jobs available to help me out. These coffee chats were really starting to put a dent in my non-existent income!

Before I knew it, years had gone by, and I was still not steamrolling on the glamorous career I had envisioned. During these bleak first years of my career, I noticed other women in the sports broadcast industry around the same age as I was experiencing unbelievable success. They skyrocketed to places like FOX Sports, ESPN, and NESN in what felt like the blink of an eye. Sitting in my parents' basement (literally, my bedroom was in their basement), it was hard not to compare my limping career to others' shiny success.

However, when I changed my perspective, I could see they were a great example of what was possible for me. Many of them were creating cutting-edge content and blazing trails for women in the sports media industry. So, I took the short-form video samples of the content they were creating and started showing them to sports media companies in my area. While admittedly there were some dark moments online comparing myself to the young, successful sports media stars, I ultimately let them shine as an example. Instead of tearing myself down, I never gave up. I stayed motivated and determined to forge my own path, even if it looked different from theirs. On that path, I landed a breakthrough role as a commercial host with FOX Sports Midwest, which led me to the position with the St. Louis Cardinals. That role skyrocketed me to CBSSports.com and subsequently the PGA TOUR, all within a few short years. My dreams had now become a reality. People started asking me where I wanted to go from there, just months into my role with the PGA TOUR. (Whoa, people! I just got here!)

I took on the mantra that there's always someone more successful than you. At first, that worked, while I enjoyed the honeymoon phase of my newly found success. But eventually I let those voices who were asking me "what's next?" creep in. Soon thereafter, those social media posts from more successful sports broadcasters and content creators started to have an effect on my attitude. Now, my dream job didn't seem good enough. I was back to comparing myself to others in similar positions. The cycle never ends. Unless you break it.

The Old Testament kings were trapped in a vicious cycle as well. Not only did they forget God and make idols of other things in their lives, but comparison was the vehicle driving many of their shortcomings. They looked at other pagan cultures around them and said, "They all have high places, so why shouldn't we?" Comparison led the Israelites to ask their kings to build the high places.

Prior to that, God came to Moses in the burning bush and tasked him with leading the Israelites out of Egypt and out of slavery to the

Promised Land. Moses and the Jews, led by God, escaped slavery, parted the Red Sea, and spent forty years in the wilderness. Their children were eventually granted the right to pass into the land flowing with milk and honey God had carved out specifically for them. They were God's people and He guided them to safety and prosperity. He gave them the Ten Commandments, which offered a guide on how to live; blessed them with food and water when they asked for it; and delivered them from enemy armies when they cried out to Him. In turn, the Israelites built Him a tabernacle, a holy tent, in which to dwell. God was their leader, He was their guide, and He was their One True King. Until they forgot about Him, in just one generation.

They started to look around at the cultures surrounding them and thought, *Hey, guys, everybody else has a king, with a crown, a throne, and royal status. They all have a man that rules their kingdom, why don't we?* Well, you have the One True God instead of a man, but you do you.

"You do you" is a phrase likely not uttered by the Israelites, but one that should give us pause today. When we see it on social media, we should immediately apply the Faith Filter and ask ourselves, is this inferring I or that person is surpassing God's will to do their own? We are called to compare ourselves to Jesus's example. When praying at the Mount of Olives on the night he was betrayed and arrested, leading to his crucifixion, Christ asked, "Father, if you are willing, remove this cup from me. Nevertheless, not my will, but yours, be done." [Luke 22:42] "You do you," in most instances today, implies the opposite. Now aware, we have the opportunity to ask ourselves, will this have a positive eternal impact? Or is this a way of justifying wrong deeds, selfish desires, or something that will not pass the Faith Filter? The rest of the Israelites story may have played out differently if they had said their version of, "God, you do you." But their story is our story and one we can apply today.

Instead, the people asked God for an earthly king. In hindsight, to us, it may seem foolish. They asked GOD to give them a man, a sinner, a lesser being, as a king, instead of the Author of the Universe. That's like your server at a nice restaurant bringing you a ribeye steak or filet mignon, and you ask them to swap it out for a hotdog instead. But God gave them what they asked for like a loving father who sometimes has to let you fall so you can learn from your bruises. God knew they would need him, and He faithfully stuck with them for this 450-plus-year lesson. We all know the path they went down: a long cycle of building high places and worshiping other gods, all because they compared themselves to hedonistic cultures around them. They willingly traded their Sovereign King for worldly rulers. Are we trading Christ as our foundation for worldly ideas on social media?

Comparison struggles didn't emerge with social media or the Israelites asking for an earthly king. Humanity has been fighting this battle since the beginning of time. Comparison is rooted in Original Sin. Being made in God's image wasn't enough for Adam and Eve; when tempted, they wanted to be God. They were just as susceptible to the enemy's lies as we are to falling under Satan's attacks of comparison today. That little voice in our heads telling us, *You should want those extravagant things, too*, or *Don't you want to be like them?* It is causing us to forget that we have been gifted a place in God's glorious kingdom that cannot be bought or earned as we scroll through social media.

That voice in our heads is the same voice that came to Eve and told her:

> "When you eat it, your eyes will be opened and you will be like God,
> knowing good and evil."
> —Genesis 3:5 CSB

"You will be like God."

The serpent lured them into the comparison trap! He made Adam and Eve think they could be like God—just like we like to make ourselves the gods of our own lives. Satan makes us think we should want all the things society puts on a pedestal, and makes us feel as though we should put ourselves on one, too. He tricks us into thinking we can have complete happiness and success if we just focus on ourselves first. If we just work hard enough, if we just look cute enough, if we just buy enough stuff—we will rule our own universe. But it's lonely in your own universe. We were created to be in union with God and each other. In fact, Eve had not yet been created when God gave Adam the command "not to eat of the tree of knowledge of good and evil" [Genesis 2:17]. Satan knew she heard this from Adam secondhand, so he used this fact to twist the truth when she was *alone*—away from Adam and vulnerable.

Just imagine Eve scrolling through social media, just like us. She sees a photo of the tree of the knowledge of good and evil and tells herself, "I don't need that forbidden fruit." The voice inside her head says, *Oh, but you could be like God.* Although Eve remembers what God told Adam, she lets another voice—the whispers of Satan—lead her astray. The enemy made her think she should want to be her own god, not just comparing herself to God but surpassing Him altogether—attempting to reinvent the role He created specifically for her.

> "God, said, 'You must not eat it or touch it, or you will die.'"
> "No! You will certainly not die," the serpent said to the woman. "In fact, God knows that when you eat it your eyes will be opened and you will be like God, knowing good and evil."
> —Genesis 3:3–5

"Ok! Let's add it to my shopping cart then."

Boom! Eve makes the purchase, and the forbidden fruit shows up overnight delivery on her doorstep the next day. Packaged, ripe, and ready for her. She opens up the box and texts a photo of it to her husband while he's at work.

"Hey Adam, check out what we're having for dinner tonight!"

"Looks great, honey! You should share that on social media so everyone else can see our awesomeness, too."

"Great idea!"

Sounds overtly silly and is obviously a modern over-distortion of what took place in Genesis 1, but that's not too far off from how I've justified some of my own social media activity.

"But those shoes are so cute." Purchase.
"But you can't see too much cleavage in that photo." Posted.
"But that person's career looks so glamorous and they seem so successful." Personal goals adjusted.

Does God want us to have all those things? Will they fill the void that He's meant to fill? Or do we just want them because we see them in other people's lives?

The Good News: God delivered the Israelites, God used Adam and Eve in big ways to set up the entire human race, and He will deliver and use you, too. He sent His only Son, the new Adam, to break that cycle of society's kings and give us a King who lives inside each of us [Romans 5:12–21]. If you've become a slave to comparison, it's not too late for you; just like it wasn't too late for me and for all of God's people. Ask Jesus to bring you out of the comparison trap, and He will.

With His help, I cast comparison aside and started letting God direct my path, and He led me to my own personal definition of success.

Turns out, His carefully chosen success for me has nothing to do with my career. His version of success has everything to do with family, love, joy, relationships, and being His disciple.

The serpent said, "You most certainly will not die."

But death of our old, self-destructive habits is the point. We want our sin, our worldly desires, the ways in which we do not follow Christ to *die*. Our old ways must die, so that we can be made new.

> "Therefore, if anyone is in Christ, he is a new creation;
> the old has passed away, and see, the new has come!"
> —2 Corinthians 5:17

Our merciful God sent His only Son as a sacrifice for us, so that we can be made new through Him. It's never too late—you are never too old or too young, too tainted or too far gone, to be made new. When you accept Jesus, you will be made new each day. If you didn't do well controlling yourself today on social media or blocking out the evil whispers, ask Him to help you and He will.

> "Ask, and it will be given to you; seek, and you will find;
> knock, and it will be opened to you."
> —Matthew 7:7

Our world puts such an emphasis on fame, followers, and likes, but as soon as your post gets countless "likes," people have already scrolled on, forgotten about your post, and someone else's post has gotten even more likes. There will always be someone with more followers, someone who comes along and goes viral next, or the newest and latest trend to follow, but your identity in Christ lasts forever. Your salvation and life beyond this earth goes on for eternity. The world of social media will forget you, but God never will. His "like" is eternal.

"And the world with its lust is passing away,
but the one who does the will of God remains forever."
—1 John 2:17

God's will is never-changing. He is "the same yesterday, today, and forever." [Hebrews 13:8] Yet, society's will and expectations are always changing. The world's goals and standards are a moving target; once you hit it, it moves again. If we compare our ambitions to the goals the world says we should have, it can be easier to go down the path of seeking ideals, lifestyles, or material items that will pass away when we do, rather than glorify God, who wants to be with us for eternity.

In today's world, we can create a social media profile, where we post the best photos of ourselves in the best moments of our lives, trying to make our highlight reel better than the next person's. Anytime we need to make ourselves feel better, we can go back to our profile and look at all our pretty pictures and the fun things that we did. We can scroll through and get ideas from other people about how to make our highlight reel better. But doesn't it ultimately feel so empty to go back through and look at our own profiles? Why do we feel a void when we focus only on ourselves, our personal success, our goals, our travels, our universe? True glory and joy comes when you don't make life about yourself.

"For we are not proclaiming ourselves but Jesus Christ as Lord,
and ourselves as your servants for Jesus's sake."
—2 Corinthians 4:5

After years of focusing only on my career, God woke me up and blessed me with a loving husband and children. I finally know what He meant by having to lose my life in order to find it. [Matthew 10:39] By finally pursuing the roles God ordained for Eve and for me, a wife and mother, I live my life for Him and for my family. I am no longer bound by the chains of total self-absorption and society's expectations. And that is a freedom only He can provide, because "if the Son sets you free, you will be free indeed." [John 8:36]

> "Christ has set us free; stand firm therefore,
> and do not submit again to a yoke of slavery."
> —Galatians 5:1

You will achieve true freedom from comparison when you apply your Faith Filter to what you consume on social media. When you realize those that are exuding the works of the flesh who you follow are enslaved to worldly desires, you, in Christ, are set free from those things. You'll suddenly see yourself on the winning side of comparison because when you have His love, you have something far greater than the newest sneaker release, coolest gadget, or trendy new sweater. You will slowly want less and less of all that, and more and more of the fruit of the Spirit.

But that type of freedom isn't easy and isn't for everyone. Many people will choose not to release themselves from those chains. You will be among the few—not the popular—when you choose freedom in Christ.

> "Enter through the narrow gate. For wide is the gate and broad is the
> road that leads to destruction, and many enter through it. But small is
> the gate and narrow the road that leads to life, and only a few find it."
> —Matthew 7:13–14

As missionary, author, and speaker Elisabeth Elliot says, "The gate is wide to make room for our selfish desires." We have so many self-centered wants, and if we reject Christ and continually give into those selfish desires, we are applauded by the world. So, not only is comparison something to be cautious about, but we need to be wary of the people we are comparing ourselves to as well. It is essential to work to vanquish this trap in our lives, because the narrow gate is what leads us to eternity with our heavenly Father.

Why is the heavenly gate so narrow? Because there is only one way through it. Jesus alone is the way. He tells us specifically, "I am the way, the truth and the life." [John 14:6]. That is why the Faith Filter is so important, because Jesus is the *only* way to eternity, and social media can distract us from the reality that the wide gate is the one that leads to Hell.

One the beauties of having Jesus, God in flesh, to dwell among us is that he is an example of someone we can all model ourselves after. Comparison can be good when drawing examples from Christ, but, nevertheless, its negative aspects are something we all have to battle. Comparison is a part of human nature. If you become aware of that, you can filter it out when comparison, not centered in Christ, tries to pop up in your life. As a Christian, you have the power to turn to the Holy Spirit to help you deal with and overcome these feelings of doubt or insecurity.

You don't have to resort to social media to wallow in your internal troubles. In fact, if you are going through a season of hardship, taking a break from social media might be your best remedy. Saturating yourself in the filtered highlight reels of others, coupled with the toxicity of some of the negative content you might inadvertently consume, could make that season in your life more difficult. There's nothing wrong with taking a break from social media, whether it's in a good season or a bad one. We all take breaks from numerous things in our lives—too much sugar, too much alcohol, too much caffeine, too much TV. There's never a bad time for a digital detox!

One simple way to detox is shared by Andy Crouch, creator of *The Tech-Wise Family*'s One-One-One Rule, which really works (I do it!):

> One hour per day,
> One day per week,
> One week per year,
> take a break from your phone.

This absence is necessary for all of us, whether you believe you have a healthy relationship with social media or not, and whether you feel comparison is something you need to work on or not. Unplugging is essential to clear your mind and give yourself the opportunity to be more present. And it is also essential to reflect on and examine your tendencies toward comparison, in order to strengthen your Faith Filter.

When you do plug back in, following Christ-centered examples— others walking in their faith, sharing theological truths, and further educating you about God—will supply you with other disciples to help bolster your own walk with Christ when you are consuming social media. God sympathizes with the reality that comparison is part of human nature, therefore the Bible calls us to not only share the gospel with nonbelievers but to also make sure we are surrounding ourselves with believers.

> "Do not be unequally yoked with unbelievers.
> For what partnership has righteousness with lawlessness?
> Or what fellowship has light with darkness?"
> —2 Corinthians 6:14

Because Jesus lightens your load by taking up the yoke beside you, partnering yourself with a large collection of believers will also make that load easier. If social media is a modern boost to fellowship and bible study, being intentional about the majority of those you follow walking with Christ will brighten your walk, too. Following faithful believers will sharpen your Faith Filter with Christ-centered comparison, that casts aside envy and evokes wisdom and encouragement.

Chapter 3 Devotional

1. Name a godly example of someone who exhibits the fruits of the Spirit in your life. Do you see them on social media?

   • What does their presence on social media look like? Does it embody the values of Christ? In what ways?

   • If they are not on social media, do you think their absence on social media plays into them being a good example? How?

2. Conversely, name an example of someone you have caught yourself admiring or longing to have what they have. Now, apply the Faith Filter.

- Do they serve as a godly example (someone who exhibits the fruits of the Spirit)?

- Or, if you think harder, are your desires to have what they have materialistic?

3. In an effort to continue to build your relationship with Jesus, bring that person's name, career, material possessions, etc., you have long wished for to Jesus in prayer. Ask the Holy Spirit to show you how to turn those desires into a goal that benefits God's Kingdom or erase them from your heart and replace them with something that draws you closer to Him.

Dear Jesus,

Please show me how my admiration of _____ can be used for *your* good.

Please replace my desires for _____ with _____ .

4. What did you put in that last blank?

5. How has that realization that you have actually been searching for _____ instead of the things that have really kept
your cup empty in your social media consumption been a
breakthrough for you?

6. Will whatever you put in those blanks fill the void that He's
meant to fill?

ONE-ONE-ONE CHALLENGE

7. This week, put down your phone for one hour per day and
one FULL day this week. Mark that full off-day on your calendar right now.

8. Keep that calendar open. Next, mark the one week this year
you are going to take off from your phone.

Prayer

Dear Lord,

You know what I need and give me strength. Help me to see the One-One-One Challenge through. That I take off one hour each day, one day each week, and one week each year from my device to become more connected to You and your creation. I realize comparison is a natural instinct, so please equally yoke me to good Christians of whom comparison will sharpen me. Forgive me for the times I've avoided your Word for the world. Focus my thoughts and efforts on others, outside of myself and break me free of the chains of total self-absorption. Therefore, ultimately redirecting my focus from down at my phone, to up to you.

Amen.

CHAPTER 4
Gratitude

As followers of Christ in God's upside-down Kingdom, He calls for us to be the opposite of what we see in society. "Love your enemies" [Matthew 5:44], "give and it will be given to you" [Luke 6:38], "whoever wants to save his life will lose it, but whoever loses his life because of me will save it," [Luke 9:24] God's power is made perfect in weakness [2 Corinthians 12:8], "Whoever exalts himself will be humbled, and whoever humbles himself will be exalted," [Matthew 23:12], and more of the backwards nature of God's glorious kingdom is outlined in the Beatitudes. To overcome the feelings of jealousy, envy, desire, or longing for the picture-perfect highlight reels we compare ourselves to on social media, we must take on a different or opposite emotion. Instead, if we are proactively grateful for what we've been given, we will then be content in our circumstances, unphased by what we see of others.

God has given us everything we need individually to carry out His plan for each of us. And with all we have been given, we are called to give back to others. We came into this world with nothing, we will leave it with nothing [1 Timothy 6:7]. The things that we value point us to where our heart lies. [Matthew 6:19–21] Does your heart lie in Jesus?

"Rejoice always, pray constantly, give thanks in everything,
for this is God's will for you in Christ Jesus."
—1 Thessalonians 5:16–18 [CSB]

Key words: "in Christ Jesus." Your gratitude starts and stops with Him. He died at Calvary so your sins would be forgiven. You owe everything to Him.

Social media will tell you that you have so much to be grateful for because *you* are awesome. We are trapped in the scrolling prison of self-absorption. As a society, we are unhappier than we've ever been because we spend all day looking *inside* instead of *up*. The gospel gives you freedom from yourself. Anything attributing to God's Kingdom, you do not get all on your own. It is through God's grace that you have anything at all, material or otherwise. We are born into sin and therefore deserve nothing, but because we have a caring and compassionate God who loves us regardless, we are able to give thanks for everything. And that means *everything* He's bestowed upon us, including the hard times. All of this is quite opposite of the messaging we see in society today. Yet God tells us through James that we should "consider it pure joy" when we "face trials of many kinds." [James 1:2]

That sounds backwards, right? How do we give thanks to a God that gives us even the hard stuff? Yes, we know we don't deserve anything [Isaiah 64:6], but hardships are still tough pills to swallow. God grants us trials because He loves us. He sharpens us and makes us better Christians by allowing obstacles to prune and shape us. But He doesn't intend for us to go through them alone. Our Father in Heaven is helping us through our troubles. If we choose to adjust our attitude by accepting the Holy Spirit into our hearts during these times, trials can draw us closer to God and help us see that we should be leaning on Him more than we usually do.

Maybe we'll never know why we're dealt some of the cards we are, but God is always there to hold our hand through them. [Isaiah 41:13] And isn't it comforting that we have the Creator of the universe holding our hand and helping us through these battles? Jesus said, "In the world you will have tribulation. But take heart; I have overcome the world." [John 16:33]

The *one* that *overcame* the world by defeating death and conquering sin is *your* helper!

Some have said that "fear not" is written 365 times in the Bible. A quick *Bible Gateway* search will show you that the words "fear" and "afraid" are used more than six hundred times in the English Standard Version. God addresses our tendencies toward fear more than 365 times! Leaving us with sweet messages of comfort nearly every time we pick up the Bible. He knows every day will be hard in its own way, so He's given us more than 365 notes of reassurance.

> "Fear not, I am the one who helps you."
> —Isaiah 41:13b

The Apostle Paul lived a wild life. His story is better than a blockbuster movie because it's true. It has it all: good vs. evil, action, suspense, and, most importantly, love. Not the romantic kind of love but an unshakable, everlasting, unapologetic love for his Lord and Savior. Paul, formerly known as Saul, was a high-ranking official and an oppressor of the worst kind, who made a living persecuting Christians. But God had bigger plans. He turned Saul into the opposite of what he once was. Saul became Paul after he encountered the Lord on the road to Damascus. The bright light of the ascended Jesus appeared on earth, delivering to Paul a message of reconciliation. Jesus's light shone so brightly, it blinded Paul for three days. He was so moved by what he experienced, in his encounter with the risen Savior and then after in the Lord healing him through Ananias, that Paul devoted his life to sharing the Good News.

What followed was a crazy ride of shipwrecks, wrestling a snake, imprisonment, great escapes, and eventually, his martyrdom. Yet, even through all the *Pirates of the Caribbean*–like action scenes, Paul never lost sight of his love for the Lord. In fact, he knew that everything he was going through was for God's great plan. And great, it was.

God used Paul to spread the gospel throughout Rome, Greece, and beyond in Paul's lifetime alone. Not to mention, Paul wrote letters to several churches and apostles in between his mission trips and his prison stays, resulting in what scholars believe to be fourteen books written by him in the New Testament. He shared in one of those letters to the Corinthian church that not just his trials, but all of theirs, would not be wasted.

> "He comforts us in all our affliction, so that we may be able to comfort those who are in any kind of affliction, through the comfort we ourselves received from God."
> —2 Corinthians 1:4

While you are in the middle of a trying time, it's likely hard to see joy and practice gratitude. But how much comfort have you gotten from helping someone else through that very trial after you've waded through it yourself? Isn't it amazing to see how God's grace is unbreakably linked to gratitude? We must never forget that it's through grace alone that we have received the most precious gift of all—our salvation [Ephesians 2:8–9]. And that alone is worth gratitude for all of eternity.

Gratitude is as much a part of the world of social media as funny cat videos and laughing babies. It's a part of the influencer dictionary, and a seemingly contractual obligation for the influencer elites to use it in their captions. At one point in the timeline of Instagram, it seemed as though nearly every influencer's post was about gratitude, they used the prayer hands emoji, or "#Blessed!" At the moment of this writing, there are 138 million Instagram posts with this hashtag. We are all definitely blessed—but something tells me these influencers wouldn't say they were blessed in their afflictions.

So, what do influencers really mean by "practicing gratitude?" For many, it's simply just being thankful for the things the universe has randomly thrown their way. Reminding others to be happy for what they have. But in truth, it's so much more than that. As a child of God, He has carefully picked each and every blessing and allowed the trials that have been bestowed on you. Like an artist meticulously mixes, creates, and chooses every color carefully for her painting, He has precisely picked gifts of love, joy, safety, success, triumph, and, yes, even allowed trials and hardships, for His masterpiece. You.

> "For you formed my inward parts; you knit me together in my mother's
> womb. I praise you, for I am fearfully and wonderfully made . . .
> in your book were written, every one of them, the days that
> were formed for me, when as yet there was none of them."
> —Psalms 139:13–14 & 16

So, as we begin to understand the deep, deep joy of realizing all of God's perfect gifts for each of us and our own unique families, we can slowly peel off the layers of comparison and instead, put on the warmth of God's grace upon us. In the end, you'll learn to practice a kind of gratitude well beyond the simple meaning of an influencer's Instagram caption.

However, the influencers do have one thing right—you have to practice it. In fact, you have to do more than just practice, you have to *choose* gratitude. It is your obligation to pick up your Bible and remind yourself and your family daily of God's grace. Although God is the great orchestrator of the universe and our lives, it is up to us to put our faith into action. We are called to *work out* our salvation [Philippians 2:12] through the process of sanctification. [1 Corinthians 1:30] And a true marker of our salvation is our desire to carry out good works [Ephesians 2:10]. Is faith without the desire to do good works really faith at all? The Bible tells us no, "faith without works is dead." [James 2:8] And works—well, they take work. Just as you hear Christian athletes thanking God for the skills they've been given and the heights to which God has taken them, those athletes have also put in hard work. We must do the same. Our faith walk takes work and it can be fueled by gratitude for the gift of God's grace.

Remember all those school assemblies you attended? When you got to skip a class so everyone in the whole school could go down to the gymnasium and file into the bleachers? Sometimes the local police department came to demonstrate CPR, or maybe, if we were really lucky, we'd get a fun assembly like a visit from zoo animals. In middle school after each of our assemblies, our principal would wrap up the show and say a few words. But, before any of us could get out of our bleacher seats to leave he would say, "Don't *have* a good day," and we'd all have to finish the phrase by shouting, "*make* a good day!" It might have been corny to some but, as a kid, I thought yelling in unison with the entire school something positive and cheerful like that was pretty cool.

"Don't have a good day, *make* a good day!"

Twenty-some years later my childhood friends and I still have that slogan ingrained in our memories. I think what our principal was trying to say is that gratitude is an action. Work is required. You actually have to put forth effort to be grateful. With God as your guiding light, *you* have to make a good day happen by intentionally adjusting your attitude and heart posture. You have to make a conscious choice to be grateful for the day and everything in it. You have to recognize your blessings, instead of wallowing in what you lack. And if it's an especially tough day, be grateful that you have Jesus to help take the wheel. (Thank you, Carrie Underwood, for popularizing my second favorite slogan.)

Each day, you must choose Jesus.

> "Do not grieve, because the joy of the Lord is your strength."
> —Nehemiah 8:10b

When you fall into the trap of comparison, gratitude becomes harder, or even fleeting. If you measure your value by the world's standards, gratitude will only last as long as it takes for you to scroll to the next post and see someone showing off their new car or a fun vacation. But we don't glorify God with the extravagant; we glorify Him in the mundane.

Jesus calls for us to take up our cross daily to follow him. What does that mean exactly? When Jesus was carrying out his ministry before his death on the cross, he traveled on foot from town to town, healing thousands of people as he went. He took questions from anyone who would approach him and healed anyone who asked. Some days that meant being bombarded by requests from every direction. Even so, can you think of any instance when Christ complained or turned someone away? No, because he did what God sent him to do—with patience, poise, and a humble heart. So, by taking up your cross daily, you are choosing Jesus as your model.

The next time you have a responsibility to do something you'd rather not do, approach it without complaint in your heart or your mind. *Make* it into a joyful task. *Make* vacuuming the floors into a blissful task, for you are glorifying the Lord by stewarding the domain He's given you. *Make* completing that checklist at work or school into a task you do gladly, because He gave it specifically to you. *Make* assisting someone else into a way to give back, rather than seeing it as a burden on you. With gratitude, we can look beyond the things that burden or inconvenience us and direct our focus to eternity. The Bible tells us not to "focus on the things that are seen but to the things that are unseen." Because the things on this earth, the things that we can see are temporary, "but what is unseen is eternal." [2 Corinthians 4:18]

Do you focus too much on what is seen? Is your focus on the trendy, the status symbols, or material things that are glorified on social media? Or are you focused on what is truly fulfilling, like following Jesus, relationships, family, and works that glorify God? That's true gratitude. And true gratitude will transform your attitude on social media.

> "But godliness with contentment is great gain. For we brought nothing into the world, and we can take nothing out of it. But if we have food and clothing, we will be content with that. Those who want to get rich fall into temptation and a trap and into many foolish and harmful desires that plunge people into ruin and destruction."
> —1 Timothy 6:6–9

Jesus tells his disciples that you cannot love God and love money, because you cannot serve two masters. [Luke 16:13] We can only achieve gratitude when we understand that our needs are not like the world's. Our happiness is not fueled by money and material things. Our happiness is fueled by Him, and He will provide us with what we need. When we shift our mindset to recognize that we are in His favor and His "like" is all we need, the gifts He grants us will then start flowing into our lives. Gifts won't just be classified by the free gifts you see content creators receiving on social media. Instead, you'll see *real* gifts all around you! Soon, you'll see each day you wake up, each breath you take, as a gift. Adjust your Faith Filter to see each homework assignment as a gift from Him, because that means you are in school growing and enriching your mind to carry out your life's work He's planned out especially for you. See each person you encounter as a gift from Him, someone you can share God's light with or as someone that can impact you. Or even a loss you've suffered, try to reflect on it—as needed or whenever possible —as a trial from Him to show that He's been right there by your side, drawing you closer to Him.

If you accept Christ, He will provide you with everything you need to carry out the tasks He brought you into this world to complete.

> "And God is able to bless you abundantly, so that in all things at all times, having all that you need, you will abound in every good work."
> —2 Corinthians 9:8 [NIV]

When we saturate ourselves in His Word daily and equally yoke ourselves to an abundance of believers on social media, we will avoid being distracted by unbiblical messages that leave us feeling ungrateful. Instead use social media as a tool to encourage you to do the good works He brought you into His Kingdom to perform. Isn't that why we are here? To carry out the good works He has lovingly ordained specifically for us? Isn't that all that we need? Isn't *He* all we need? Adjusting to put God at the forefront of our hearts is what will empower us to *make* every day good. When His "like" is all we truly need, God in His fullness of grace, glory and goodness is what motivates us to *practice* gratitude.

Chapter 4 Devotional

1. Name something difficult that you have been through in the past. From that experience, how have you learned, grown, or seen it change into something good years later?

2. How can you use that difficulty to help someone else going through something similar now?

3. Name something difficult you are going through right now.

4. Ask God to a) help you through it, b) use it for something good, and c) to give you peace in not knowing what the fruits of this current trial might produce.

5. Look up these "Fear Not" verses: (Write out the one(s) that speak to your heart.)
   - Matthew 10:31
   - John 12:15
   - Luke 12:32
   - Isaiah 43:5
   - Genesis 15:1
   - Isaiah 41:16
   - Revelation 1:17
   - Isaiah 54:4

6. Pause for a moment. What is something that you wish you would've done or handled better today or yesterday?

7. How would taking a breath and choosing Jesus change how you handled that situation or mental downfall? (How can you *make* it better the next time by intentionally coming to the situation with gratitude?)

8. What is something mundane that you have grown to resent or dislike?

9. Why do you think God has given you that task? How does that task help serve His Kingdom?

10. How can you approach that task next time with gratitude? Or redirect your service to something else that does serve His Kingdom?

FAITH FILTER CHALLENGE

11. This week, when you are driving somewhere as a family or alone, say three things out loud that each of you are thankful for.

12. Then, each of you name a person to pray for and go around the car praying for that person.

Not only is this a challenge to practice gratitude but it's also to help aid you to be more intentional. Instead of zoning out to a podcast or your kids being glued to their phones, while in the car, naturally unplug from your device and tune in to each other and the common bond of our Lord and Savior.

Prayer

Dear Lord,

Words cannot describe how grateful I am for You, your grace, mercy and patience. Forgive me for my self-absorbed frustration at the mundane tasks I've failed to notice are handed down by You. Help me to realize, in the moment, the tasks I have grown to resent are divine assignments given by You. Help me to focus on the things that are unseen. Remind me as I begin each morning that I should set out to MAKE it into a day that glorifies you. Readjust what I treasure, so I can understand what needs are truly important for me to carry out your kingdom work with a joyful heart.

Amen.

Chapter 5

Soul Influence

An influencer is defined by Merriam-Webster Dictionary as, "a person who is able to generate interest in something (such as a consumer product) by posting about it on social media." Their promotional efforts are as good as their reach. The more people that follow them, the more people they can potentially influence to purchase products, translating to more commissions. Therefore, the emphasis on acquiring followers has become a goal many aspire to in hopes of obtaining popularity, some sort of social media fame or influencer income. The role of an influencer has become coveted.

Traditionally, when you'd ask a kid what they wanted to be when they grew up, they'd say a doctor, a teacher, whatever their parents do, etc. Today, when you ask them, they may tell you a YouTube star or a social media influencer. This career aspiration has only recently come about, leaving many still possibly asking themselves, *Is that even a real job?*

Yes. Yes, it is. Just like being a starting forward on an NBA roster is a job. And just like it takes years of hard work to become a professional athlete, it does take hard work to be an elite influencer with hundreds of thousands of followers; with the exception that you don't have to be seven feet tall, and going viral can happen instantly.

Despite what many people think, crafting, planning, and composing social media posts takes skill and likely more time and effort than you'd think to allocate. Furthermore, it's a job that never ends: the internet is always going, 24/7, and influencers have to stay relevant 365 days of the year.

"But, hey! Wait a second! I'm a mom, my job never ends, either!"

"I'm a student, I have to stay on top of my studies around the clock too!"

"I'm a business owner. My company, clients, and employees need me even during my off time!"

You are *so* right! What if I told you, *you* are an influencer? This might be about the time you laugh and say something like, "But I don't know how to do social media," or "But I don't have thousands of followers." Maybe not. But you have influence. While someone with millions of followers at the top of their Instagram game may have far more reach than you do, you potentially have more influence on people's *souls*, particularly those around you—your friends, your family, your loved ones.

And aren't those the most important people? You have influence on their eternal standing with our Creator, their views on themselves as children of God, and their place in the Kingdom.

Merriam-Webster also defines an influencer, "as a person who guides the actions of others." That is all of us. The maximum influence we have is on the people immediately around us. That is our battleground; that's our calling. And God has given us the ultimate tool of the Bible to carry out His work.

"All Scripture is breathed out by God and profitable for teaching, for reproof, for correction, and for training in righteousness, that the man of God may be competent, equipped for every good work."
—2 Timothy 3:16–17

"Iron sharpens iron" and we sharpen each other. [Proverbs 27:17]

Through my more than a decade's work as a sports broadcaster, I've been blessed to build up a social media following, which we are grateful has allowed me to make a little income for my family and hopefully have a positive impact on others. My most important job, however, is what God has assigned me with: sharpening my family at home, my family at church, my friends, neighbors, and the people immediately around me.

Too often we find ourselves thinking we must change the world in a big way, that we need to have a large influence on society. But the biggest impact we have is on our small circle—our family. We aren't called to affect the whole world; we're called to take care of our space in this world. The best way you can make the world a better place is by starting small. If you are a mom or dad, start with your family. If you are single, start with your friends or your inner circle within your community. Will you look at yourself as a soul influencer, as He does? We are all pieces in God's puzzle. Take care of your piece and He'll put the rest together.

We see throughout scripture how influence impacts each and every story God has shared with us. We've already talked about some of those examples: the influence Eve had on her husband to eat the forbidden fruit; the influence the kings had on their kingdoms; the influence the kings' wives had on their ruling husbands to worship other gods and build the high places for them. As you can tell, those are all examples of what *not* to do. Jesus poignantly warns us about negative influence and holding on to our sinful ways.

"Remember Lot's wife!"
—Luke 17:32

"Lot's wife" is how we know her, because her name isn't recorded in scripture. We have to flip all the way back to the very first book in the Bible, Genesis, to read about her cautionary story of influence.

Lot was Abraham's cousin (the Abraham that God promised to give more descendants than stars in the sky; [Genesis 26:4] the Abraham through which God established Jesus's line and family tree, making him the Messiah's ancestor).

When Abraham and Lot left Egypt to settle elsewhere, they came to the plain of the Jordan. Abraham gave Lot the option to settle his camp wherever he wanted. [Genesis 13:9] Despite Sodom and Gomorrah's bad reputation as a region full of sin and evil, Lot chose to settle there anyway because it appeared to be well-watered and fruitful.

You likely have heard the names Sodom and Gomorrah. They've made their way into popular vernacular, never used in a positive context. The city full of sexual immorality, violence and sin, reflects what we can see today in the darkest depths of the "hidden evils" online. Nevertheless, just like some are tempted to venture there today, Lot took his camp, livestock, and herds to Sodom and Gomorrah.

Several years later, God sent angels to destroy the cities to wipe out their evil ways. The Lord took mercy on Lot and said he would save his family if they fled. On the night the angels came, Lot took them into his house, to save them from an angry mob in the city. To stave off the crowd, Lot suggested his two young daughters as a peace offering. Luckily, the crowd said no.

Where was Lot's wife during this episode? Perhaps she had little or no power over her husband's choices, but as we've noted from the various examples so far, women can have an impact on their husbands. So, whether it's direct impact on their husband's decisions in the moment, like we've noted with Eve and the wives that persuaded their husband-kings to worship other gods and build high places, or it's an indirect influence that can have an impact on their family's decisions—I can't help but ask the question, where was Lot's wife?

One would like to think that, no matter the negative influence she experienced all around her, she would still choose the righteous path when her moment came, much like Abigail did in 1 Samuel 25 when her proud husband refused to nourish David and his army. Abigail, without hesitation, took the future king of Israel the food he needed and with a humble heart asked him to spare her husband and leave their family in the hands of God.

However, Abigail's story of faith and humility is in contrast with Lot's wife. The angels destroyed that insane mob and terrible city, while Lot and his family fled. With one caveat, "Run for your lives! Don't look back! And don't stop anywhere on the plain! Run to the mountains, or you will be swept away!" [Genesis 19:17] Given the trajectory of the story, you can likely predict what Lot's wife did next. As they were running for their lives and Sodom and Gomorrah were set on fire from above, she looked back.

> "But Lot's wife looked back and became a pillar of salt."
> —Genesis 19:26

By looking back, Lot's wife was, in some way, longing for the land full of sinful, enticing, and tempting practices. She was looking back at her former life, instead of forward at a new life, one where she and her family could be made new.

*"'Remember Lot's wife!' He said. 'Whoever tries to keep their life will
lose it, and whoever loses their life will preserve it.'"*
—Luke 17: 32–33

The rest of her family were given, by God, the chance to make their lives new, to not look back at their former life of sin and long for it, but instead, walk with arms wide open into a new life where they could, little-by-little, through grace and santification, be made new and righteous. From what the Bible tells us happened next, the rest of Lot's family did not choose the path of being made new. Whatever the influence in their lives, whether it was Sodom and Gomorrah, their mother, their father, or some combination, they clearly chose to reject God and remain in sin.

However, we do know that no matter how much we have been in sin or what negative influence we've had in our lives, Jesus can rescue and redeem us if we accept him as our Lord and Savior. He's not just asking us not to look back, but to also accept him with a new heart, eyes fixed on him. And when we do stumble, He reminds us He'll be waiting there with grace, mercy, and a host of positive examples of influence to encourage us in scripture. [Matthew 11:29]

Because influence on the people around you is everything! Just as we see in the juxtaposition of Lot's Wife versus Abigail.

Influence is so important, numerous positive stories of God's people impacting others are woven throughout the Bible as lessons of wisdom for us. Like the story of Queen Esther, who saved her people from the decree of the king (her husband) of Persia, one of the greatest empires of the world. Esther convinced him to spare the lives of the Jews in his empire by putting her life on the line. [Esther 7:3–4] Now that's walking the path of righteousness by faith!

There is also the story of Mary Magdalene, whose demons were removed by Christ and in her gratitude, she devoted her entire life to following him during his ministry on earth. [Luke 8:1–2] She not only had an unmeasurable influence during his earthly ministry efforts as one of his close supporters and followers, but she was also the first to see Jesus after he was resurrected from the tomb and understand that he was the Risen Savior. Her faith led her to be the messenger to the twelve disciples that Jesus had risen from the dead, sparking the movement of Christianity and the spread of Christ's church throughout the world. [John 20:18] These are just a few of many examples.

While most of us probably will not save our entire race from an emperor or lead our family down such an evil path as Lot's, we can ask the Lord on a daily basis to help guide us and give us the strength, faith, and discipline to lean in like Mary Magdalene.

> "See if there is any offensive way in me,
> and lead me in the way everlasting."
> —Psalm 139:24

Challenging points in our lives, like trying to get through school or raising a family, can expose the worst in us. Stress can lead us to quips of anger or lapses in judgment—right at the very time that our positive influence is needed the most. But God is using those moments to show us the areas in our hearts that need the most improvement. He uses everything for good, to influence and impact our hearts, so we can then have a positive, eternal impact on others —a soul influence.

I, myself, am quick to anger. It bubbled up as a student, when technology didn't function the way I needed it to. It festered as a young professional, lacking the patience to let my career take its God-ordained course, getting flustered at every bump in the road. It was exposed when I married a man whose exemplary patience showed the lack of my own. And it was brought front and center when I became a mom, working, running a household, and taking care of babies and toddlers.

My patience was like a rubber band stretched out so tight, it was ready to snap at any moment. But I knew God was trying to show me that this was an area I could improve. An area that if I did better, it would make me a better person and a better influence in my children's lives. I also knew, He would help me. When I was desperately searching, He led me to read this question in a study on James by John MacArthur[3]:

> "How would it change your life today (specifically and practically)
> if you could remember in each moment that the old you is dead
> and that God has given you a new nature [2 Cor. 5:17],
> one that loves God and hates sin?"

Wow! Now I was given the tool to turn to *Him* when I lost my patience. When my computer died and the charger wouldn't work because my daughter, with a poopy diaper, chewed on the end of it, right as I was logging into a virtual meeting—all at the same time I was cooking dinner, while my husband was gone for work—I'd normally lose my cool over something like this. But MacArthur's thought-tool allowed me to realize in that moment that I desperately needed the Lord's help, instead of turning to my own bad habits.

In that instance I thought to myself, *How would Jesus show patience and kindness right now?* That points us back to the famous bumper sticker from the nineties: WHAT WOULD JESUS DO? It seems so cliché. But it works! We ask ourselves that because he is perfect and is our ultimate example of how to live righteously. Jesus is the ultimate influencer. And he is ultimately who we should look to in every aspect of our lives, even our social media habits. He influences us, so we can positively influence others.

Sharing bible verses on social media isn't your thing? That's ok! To carry out the good works God has assigned specifically for us to do, to break out of the trap of comparison, to be grateful for both the trials and the joys he's given you, to be a soul influencer—you don't have to broadcast it on social media. (Though, that would be fine, too!) In fact, Jesus tells us the Lord rewards the work we put in with Him privately.

> "But when you pray, go into your room, close the door and
> pray to your Father, who is unseen. Then your Father,
> who sees what is done in secret, will reward you."
> —Matthew 6:6

You don't have to broadcast your faith to the masses, people will just know. If you live out your faith, people will recognize that there's something different about you. Something that they want, more than the fancy "stuff" and the popular Instagram page. Your life will naturally have that intangible Faith Filter and you will have a positive influence on others. Influence you might not even be aware of.

Jesus shares with his disciples that people will know who they are, if they love one another. [John 13:35] So, no matter how much you may want to keep your faith private, it will shine through. Just like you can't prevent a light from shining in the darkness. [Luke 8:16 & 11:33] You are a soul influencer. Realize that you have that light in you, so you can look to Jesus to help refine it and, in turn, share it with others.

Chapter 5 Devotional

1. Read Matthew 6:1–4. In what ways do you see social media reflected in those verses?

2. Let's dive into what the rewards are that Jesus shares in these passages.
   - (v. 2) "Thus, when you give to the needy, sound no trumpet before you, as the hypocrites do in the synagogues and in the streets, that they may be praised by _____ . Truly, I say to you, they have received their reward."
   - (v. 3–4) "But when you give to the needy, do not let your left hand know what your right hand is doing, so that your giving may be in secret. And your _____ who sees in secret will reward you."
   - The reward is from _____

3. In what ways does society today feel like or reflect Sodom and Gomorrah?

4. We quoted 2 Timothy 3:16–17 in the book but look back at the previous verses 12–13.

- Does it feel like if you turn from the ways of the modern Sodom and Gomorrah you described above, you will be persecuted?

- Do you let that impact your influence?

- What implications could that have, according to verse 13?

5. BUT verse 11 in 2 Timothy 3 delivers good news. It states, "my persecutions and sufferings that happened to me . . . from them all the Lord _____ me."

- How does that change your perspective?

FAITH FILTER CHALLENGE

6. Who, around you, do you have the most influence on?

7. Do others publicly see that influence?

8. Does it matter that others do or don't publicly see that influence?

9. What ways can you impact their soul? (For example, their eternal standing in God's kingdom, their love and acceptance of Jesus as their Savior or to exhibit fruits of the spirit in times of trial.)

Declare yourself a soul influencer.
I am a soul influencer because God has put _____
in my life so I can impact them by _____.

10. What shortcoming is the Lord currently exposing in your life?

11. Answer John MacArthur's question:
"How would it change your life today (specifically and practically) if you could remember in each moment that the old you is dead and that God has given you a new nature [2 Cor. 5:17], one that loves God and hates sin?"

12. How can you use this tool moving forward?

Prayer

Dear Lord,

Thank you for forgiving and exposing my weaknesses, so that I may become stronger. Please speak to me in the moments that I fall short or get frustrated, to remind me that I am a new person in Christ, thanks to You. Thank You for giving me influence on others. Show me the tools to use that influence and impact another's soul. Lord, guide me to have an eternal impact on [list names here]:

Give me the wisdom to be the soul influencer You created me to be.

Amen.

CHAPTER 6

The Ultimate Influencer

Jesus was the original influencer. He is the first and the last—the Number 1 influencer we should look to. [Revelation 22:13] Jesus has influenced billions of people in the two thousand years since his death. No other person even comes close. Jesus invented the "follow" button and instructs us to follow him more than twenty times in the Gospels.

Two of the most beautiful words ever uttered in scripture: "Follow me."

It's an invitation so sweet, the disciples dropped everything they were doing in that very moment to hit that follow button. Would you?

> "Follow me, and I will make you fishers of men."
> —Matthew 4:19

Simon (Peter) and his brother Andrew were fishermen by trade. In the middle of a workday, trying to provide food for their family, their community, and their Jewish counterparts, a man they did not know walked up to their boat, seemingly out of nowhere, and asked them to follow him. They dropped their nets right there, without hesitation, and followed Jesus. Then Jesus, Simon, and Andrew walked a bit further and saw brothers James and John tending to their fishermen duties with their father Zebedee. Again, that invitation came!

"Follow me."

And they did! Scripture says James and John "immediately left the boat and their father and followed him." [Matthew 4:22] That's a powerful follow button! Right there, on the spot, the brothers left their job and their father to follow Jesus. They abandoned their fresh cup of coffee from the breakroom, didn't turn off their computer or push in their chair—just got up from their desk, left, and never came back. They didn't even give their boss two weeks' notice! (How many have daydreamed of doing that?!)

This is a far cry from today's follow button, where you just hit "follow" and then continue to swipe through your feed without any disruption to your day. These disciples left their families, their jobs, their homes, to walk hundreds of miles on the roads of Israel with a man they didn't know but knew in their hearts was about to change the world for all of eternity. Who doesn't want to follow that?! Jesus's profile wasn't private. You didn't have to send him an invitation on Instagram for him to later "approve" and allow you to view his page. Anyone could and can follow Jesus, if they hear and respond to his call. Anyone.

Matthew is a beautiful example of how *anyone* can be called to follow Jesus. Matthew, who wrote the first book of the Gospel, was originally a tax collector in Jesus's day, during the Roman reign over Palestine. Tax collectors at that time were hated, and seen as sinners, taking money from their own Jewish people and giving it to the enemy and ruling Romans. But Jesus still uttered those two words to Matthew while sitting at his tax booth:

"Follow me."

Leaving everything behind, Matthew immediately stopped working, got up from his chair, and followed him, scripture tells us. [Luke

8:28] Maybe you aren't a tax collector, but we are certainly all sinners. Just like the original disciples, we are all fishing for someone to save us from our collection of sins.

Our savior has a public profile, he's asking you to hit that follow button. In fact, it's the most important "follow" you will ever make. It not only shapes your life and the lives of those around you, but it will determine where you spend eternity. And eternity is a really long time! The world emphasizes how many followers we have, but in God's eyes, it's Who we follow that's important. If you deny yourself, taking off the bondage of worldly standards, and pick up your cross by choosing Jesus daily as your ultimate influencer, you will be following the only One that matters. [Matthew 16:24, Luke 9:23]

Fortunately for us, Jesus has an instruction manual on how to follow him. One that goes much deeper than pretty square pictures or fifteen-second videos of him dancing. (Just imagine Jesus on TikTok for a second.) We often find ourselves trying to emulate those that we follow on social media. Buying the clothes they wear; going to the places they suggest; implementing the workout or swing tips they give you to improve your golf game. Why do we work so hard to follow along with what we see on social media, yet we don't try nearly as hard to live by Jesus's example?

Looking at this question spiritually, the answer is that social media is an easy tool for the enemy. Yes, Satan is real, and yes, he uses anything he can to distract us from our true purpose—following Jesus. And he doesn't have to work very hard to distract us anymore. Social media does all the work for him! We, all too easily (myself included), fall into the trap of seeing that little red mark, indicating we have a notification on social media, opening up the app, and losing ourselves in meaningless content for much longer than we intended.

According to LogOffMovement.org, sixteen- to twenty-four-year-olds spend an average of 180 minutes on social media per day. Too much unproductive time spent on our devices is time the enemy gained, and our Lord and Savior lost. And we gave it to him, willingly. That's time we could've spent being productive in the Word.

(Tip: Download a Bible app, such as my favorite, the YouVersion Bible App to open up instead when you get the urge to scroll. You could also try the ESV Study Bible or Gideon Bible App. Reference the chapter devotional to see how you can set a time limit on social media or other apps and how to gain insights into your time spent per day online.)

We could've spent that time helping others or glorifying God through the mundane tasks He set out for us to do that day. (Yes, He wants you to clean your room and make your bed. They glorify Him by taking care of the world He created for *you*.) Once we start seeing our time as valuable minutes the Lord gives us to follow Him and do His work—and seeing our extra, unproductive social media consumption time as distractions the enemy has set out for us—it can help us be more conscious of the time we spend following Jesus versus the time we spend falling into Satan's traps. Time is a valuable commodity, a gift from the Lord. None of us know how much time we have on this earth. Do you want to spend the majority of that looking at your screen? Or carrying out God's work? I pray you voted for the latter. Because Jesus died so you could follow him.

God sent his only Son to be slandered, tortured, hung on a cross, and slowly executed so that you could choose to follow him and not Satan, so that you could have eternal life and live out his influence. And he willingly endured all of that because he loves you. Because *He* chose *you* to glorify His eternal kingdom. [John 3:16]

Right here, right now, as you read this book, you can make that decision to follow Jesus instead of just social media. It's not going to be easy; you'll have to fight off the urge to aimlessly scroll and waste large amounts of your time. It's also going to require some reading. (Sorry!) And it will require you to redirect your focus away from your screen toward the earth and the people He has set before you. (Whew! You can escape your phone!) But I will warn you, in a positive light, that following Jesus as your main influencer will cause you to see things differently.

Your lens is going to start to shift from the things that are seen to "the things that are unseen. For the things that are seen are transient, but the things that are unseen are eternal." [2 Corinthians 4:18] As Christians, we are set apart. The Bible says, "you are a chosen race, a royal priesthood, a holy nation, a people for his own possession, that you may proclaim the excellencies of him who called you out of the darkness into his marvelous light." [1 Peter 2:9] We are not to "be conformed to this world, but be transformed by the renewal of your mind, that by testing you may discern what is the will of God, what is good and acceptable and perfect." [Romans 12:2] Not just for the sake of being different, but for Him. And if we do all things for Him, we will surely benefit and so will others (helping others is the best part)!

> "I can do all things through him who strengthens me."
> —Philippians 4:13

Truly knowing our Lord and Savior, and our Father who sent him, will allow you to follow Him more easily and readily each day. Studying Him, diving into scripture, and reading about what makes Him tick are all ways to draw closer to the Lord. In the same way getting to know a friend, spouse, or family member more deeply will allow you to become closer to them.

As a family or individual, one of the easiest ways to get to know God is through Catechisms—questions and answers about the various intricacies of our Creator. All it takes is reading one question and answer from a Catechism book at the breakfast table (or whenever works for you or your family as a group). We enjoy the New City Catechism and have a kid's version we do together with our little ones. No matter how busy you are, if you can make time to scroll through your phone, you can make time for one question and answer to connect, as a family, with God. By connecting with Him, you are following the Ultimate Influencer.

His follow button isn't a passive pursuit, it's an active answer to God's calling. Even though we are called not to be like the world, we are still in this world—so how should we act? We can observe through scripture how Jesus acts in certain situations and, therefore, how we are called to act in the same manner.

He outlines the attributes of a Christian, one-by-one, in the Beatitudes in his Sermon on the Mount. If Jesus were on YouTube, the Sermon on the Mount would likely be his most viewed video of all-time. It's Jesus's influence 101 or, if you are an eighties baby like me, *Christianity for Dummies*. If you haven't heard of or studied the Beatitudes until this moment, don't feel bad. I breezed right through them the handful of times I read or heard them, until I listened to a podcast on them, which of course means I'm now an expert on this topic—just like you will be after you read this chapter.

All jokes aside, this is what happens when we are in the world more than in the Word! Surrounding ourselves with content to make us more informed Christians rather than content that continuously distracts or stimulates us is so important! Don't get me wrong, Golden Retrievers of Instagram is an entertaining social media account. Fun content is fine, but we must be conscious about how much we take ourselves away from His teachings, or when we conform to what we see from non-Christians. Society seems to be teaching us to be the opposite of the attributes Jesus plainly describes for us that make a good Christian, which is why the Beatitudes may seem odd to the world today.

> "Blessed are the poor in spirit, for theirs is the kingdom of heaven."
> —Matthew 5:3

Who wants to be poor? What does that even mean? If you scroll through your Instagram feed today, poor is definitely not something you'll see. Wealth is glamorized and something people not only aspire to have but flaunt it. However, much of the "wealth" you see on social media is contrived. The abundance of products that influencers display are, by-and-large, given to them; many times they didn't purchase all the *stuff* that they are paid to show off.

That's not actually what Jesus is referring to in this first line of his Sermon on the Mount. He's talking about being poor in a figurative sense, not in a worldly manner. He's telling us those who know that they have nothing and are nothing without Him will ascend to Heaven. We are inadequate sinners that cannot do or accomplish anything for God's Kingdom without him by our side. To "follow" him, we must acknowledge our shortcomings as descendants of Adam and Eve, who rerouted humanity into being sinners. That's all of us, and we all are nothing without Jesus.

Wow, that likely wouldn't get you any "likes" on social media. In fact, you see the complete opposite getting reposted and shared and glorified continuously. Self-reliance is preached, self-care is an industry, and selfish pursuits are mainstream. Everywhere you turn people are telling you to rely on yourself, that "the power" is deep inside you. You can do anything if you just look inside yourself and tap into your inner strength.

That's a lie. A lie Satan loves for us to believe.

Not to mention, how much pressure is that?! We weren't intended to do it all on our own. And who wants to? Today, we see people collapsing at a high rate under the immense pressure to do everything themselves, to chase success, fueled by self-reliance. Forty-five percent of teens feel overwhelmed according to LogOffMovement.org and thirteen-year-old girls, who spend an average of one to two hours on social media per day, were at a higher risk of suicide, which is the second leading cause of death among young people according to the CDC.[4] Our youth and people in general are desperately searching for help.

Binding yourself to someOne or someThing else and considering it freedom may sound like an oxymoron. Surrendering the mindset, *I can do it on my own*, and renewing your thoughts to believe that you can do it *with* Jesus is the most freeing feeling in the world. In fact, it's part of what "being saved" means. "For freedom Christ has set us free." We are no longer slaves to sin, but through Christ's death on the cross and his call for us to follow him, we are set free from the penalty and power of sin. [Galatians 5:1] When you have that realization that you are saved from the eternal consequences of your sin and that the power of the Holy Spirit can help you overcome any sin in your life, you will feel like a new person. The weight of the world will melt away. Jesus wants you to follow him, to take that weight off your shoulders.

> "They promise them freedom, but they themselves are slaves of corruption, since people are enslaved to whatever defeats them."
> —2 Peter 2:19 CSB

Early in my social media and broadcast days, I lived to glorify myself instead of God and Christ's Church. So, no matter how my career advanced, the glory wasn't good enough—because it was selfish. I wanted to be famous in sports media. I would do almost anything it took to be successful in my industry. I was doing it based on Christian morals. I was doing it honestly, being nice to others. I even ignored one of my boss's suggestions to wear tighter shirts and show more cleavage. So, I had to be doing it correctly, right?

Wrong. I was leaving out the Ultimate Influencer.

The Bible does call us to work hard, don't ever stop doing that. But your work should be for His glory, not your own. Each time I got a new opportunity, I thought it was going to be great, but it never turned out to be exactly how I had imagined it. I was doing it for me, for my glory alone.

On a rollercoaster of a career-path, I ended up in Jacksonville, Florida, as the on-camera host for the PGA TOUR. As a golf enthusiast, that is a dream job—one I never set my sights on. It was God's plan all along to plant me in Ponte Vedra Beach, where I would thrive in reporting on a sport I grew up playing, marry my husband, start a family, and become part of a church that would strengthen our faith. None of that was part of my plan! But it was His and it was much more beautiful than my own.

Too often we forget about God and think only of our plan instead of walking in faith and praying for His direction every step of the way. We should crave His guidance, His total influence on our lives. Because the God of the universe—the God who created the heavens and the earth, who has orchestrated everything to happen in the past, present, and future—can craft a more magnificent plan for our lives than our minds are able to foresee.

> "'For I know the plans I have for you,' declares the Lord, 'plans for welfare and not for evil, to give you a future and a hope.'"
> —Jeremiah 29:11

See, welfare! (Prosperity, good-fortune, happiness.) He wants that for you! But you can only find gain through godliness with contentment [1 Timothy 6:6] by recognizing your poverty first. All the other Christian attributes Jesus lays out in the Beatitudes in the Sermon on the Mount depend on this. They depend on you depending on Jesus.

What was the second part of that first Beatitude again? "Blessed are the poor in spirit, *for theirs is the kingdom of Heaven*." Don't you want to spend eternity with the Father living in a perfect paradise? Just like this one, the secondary part of each Beatitude reveals rewards that I think most anyone (Christian or not) would want—things like being comforted and satisfied, seeing God, and going to heaven. But we can show others through our light on social media that being blessed with comfort, satisfaction, and eternal glory comes from the lessons we glean from the Ultimate Influencer.

"Blessed are the poor in spirit → for theirs is the kingdom of heaven.
Blessed are those who mourn → for they shall be comforted.
Blessed are the meek → for they shall inherit the earth.
Blessed are those who hunger and thirst for righteousness →
for they shall be satisfied.
Blessed are the merciful → for they shall receive mercy.
Blessed are the pure in heart → for they shall see God.
Blessed are the peacemakers → for they shall be called sons of God.
Blessed are those who are persecuted for righteousness' sake →
for theirs is the kingdom of heaven.
Blessed are you when others revile you and persecute you and utter all
kinds of evil against you falsely on my account → Rejoice and be glad,
for your reward is great in heaven, for so they persecuted the prophets
who were before you."
[Matthew 5:3–12]

The Beatitudes can serve as an outline from Jesus, The Ultimate Influencer himself, on how to use social media as a tool in our Christian walk. Social media can be a place to come alongside people who are mourning. [Matthew 5:4] Message them, ask how you can pray for them, or deliver a meal to them. Use it as a way to connect with them in their time of need and reflect Christ's compassion. Meek, or humility, is now spreading on social media, as people help others by sharing the skills or knowledge they have acquired, possibly to create something for their home, a recipe or gardening tip. [Matthew 5:5] Rather than just showing off the end result boastfully, people are now equipping others to carry out new tasks or learn new skills, too.

More Christians are embracing sharing their worldview. [Matthew 5:10–12] Though I don't think I can find "I'm blessed for being reviled and persecuted" anywhere on Kim Kardshian's twitter feed, others are finally saying, "though it may be unpopular by Hollywood's standards, living a Christian life is more fulfilling. Here is how I am doing it." When we weigh the messages from those we follow against His standards, like the Beatitudes, we can be more confident that the content we are taking in (hopefully in moderation), from various social media personalities can help create a community of Christ-centered encouragement around us on our devices.

When you follow Jesus, it doesn't matter how many followers you have or what skills you possess, he'll perform miracles in your life if you look for them. During Jesus's life on earth, he performed so many miracles they couldn't write them all down. [John 20:30] The miracles the authors of the Gospels chose to include show us the wide variety of people he impacted. Maybe you will see yourself in some of the biblical examples scripture provides, or you will be reminded of someone in your life that the Ultimate Influencer inspires you to recognize your potential soul influence in their life.

In one specific instance, Jesus was on his way to perform a miracle for a well-known man in the community. The synagogue leader's daughter was on her deathbed, and he called on Jesus to revive his daughter. The crowds followed Jesus on his way to this very important task for a very important family. However, the Bible makes a point to tell us about a woman in that crowd that had been bleeding for twelve years. [Mark 5:25] The woman came up, touched Jesus's clothes as he was making his way through the crowd, and was healed. Jesus stopped, feeling power come out of him, and proceeded to ask who had touched his clothes, listen to her heartbreaking story of suffering, and put his task for an important family on pause.

If you feel like Jesus isn't at work in your life like he might appear to be in someone else's on social media, remember and study this woman. Her affliction wasn't just for a few days or once a month. No, she had been menstruating for twelve straight years. Every day, she was in isolation, cutoff from everyone. In the Jewish community, she was considered unclean. She wasn't able to come in contact with anyone and was not permitted to go into the synagogue or even to live in town. This lady didn't just have zero followers; she had a negative next to her number. All the friends and family she once had were no longer in her life, but Jesus still gave her a miracle. On his way to help a very important person, he made time for the woman everyone had forgotten about.

> "'Daughter,' he said to her, 'your faith has saved you.
> Go in peace and be healed from your affliction.'"
> —Mark 5:34

What tender words from the Son of God. That is the only time in scripture Jesus calls a woman "daughter."[5] And he reserved that term of endearment for an outcast—over a man's daughter of high standing that he went on to help raise from the dead. So, whether you feel important like that man's family, or down in the depths like that daughter of Christ, if you believe in him, if you follow the Ultimate Influencer, miracles are waiting for you.

Chapter 6 Devotional

1. What was your "follow me" moment with Jesus? If you are in a group study, share with your group.

2. Jesus *died* for that "follow me" moment you just described. How does this make you feel?

3. What ways have you tried to adapt or change yourself to be like what you see on social media?

4. What ways, instead, can you adapt yourself to be more like Jesus?

5. How many times per day or week do you look at media on your device?

TRACKING CHALLENGE

6. Check your screen time on your phone and write down how much time you've spent in your top five "Most Used" apps. If you have an iPhone, go into "Settings," search "Screen Time." Under the Daily Average chart, click "See All Activity" and the "Week" tab.

Tip: Also under "Screen Time" in your iPhone, click "App Limits" and set a time limit on your most-used app that is less than your current average daily time use.

TIP	App	Time
1.		
2.		
3.		
4.		
5.		

- How many times per day or week do you read the Bible? (Be honest!)

- Based on those answers, do you "follow" Jesus or social media more?

7. This coming week, aim to read the Bible and spend time in prayer *more* than you do on social media.

   To reach that goal I need to spend _____ time with Jesus and in the Word *versus* _____ amount of time I normally spend on social media. (As recorded in the Time Tracking Challenge on page 86.)

Tip: For an easy way to track your time, use your favorite Bible app. Then your phone will track your time for you. At week's end, go back into "Screen Time" and record your time.

   Time spent on the Bible app: _____
   Time spent on all other apps: _____

Or, if you want to ditch the temptations on your device, track it here by hand!

	Time in the word	Time on my phone
Day 1		
Day 2		
Day 3		
Day 4		
Day 5		
Day 6		
Day 7		

Prayer

Dear Lord,

Thank You for sending your only Son to die a gruesome death on the cross, so that I might live out his influence today. Show me the ways that I am not fully "following" Jesus. Expose the areas I can grow and follow him more intimately. Help me to learn from the Ultimate Influencer so that I may be a soul influencer to others.

Amen.

Chapter 7

Discernment

When you follow Jesus Christ as your ultimate influencer, it will no longer be a miracle for you to conquer that which plagues you on social media. Christ is your chain breaker. Sin will no longer have you in its shackles. The Ultimate Guide is now by your side helping to fight these battles for you. [John 16:13, Hebrews 13:16, Psalm 28:7] The Holy Spirit will equip you with the tools you need to continue using social media, by navigating it from a place of freedom as a new person in Christ. From there, arm yourself with Armor of God each time you login to your favorite platform.

> "Therefore, put on the full Armor of God, so that when the day of evil comes, you may be able to stand your ground, and after you have done everything, to stand. Stand firm then, with the belt of truth buckled around your waist, with the breastplate of righteousness in place, and with your feet fitted with the readiness that comes from the gospel of peace. In addition to all this, take up the shield of faith, with which you can extinguish all the flaming arrows of the evil one. Take the helmet of salvation and the sword of the Spirit, which is the word of God.
>
> And pray in the Spirit on all occasions with all kinds of prayers and requests. With this in mind, be alert and always keep on praying for all the Lord's people."
> —Ephesians 6:10–18 NIV

As you continue to dive into scripture and learn more and more about God, you will hone your Faith Filter to become more saturated in truth. Soon you will then develop discernment—the ability to decipher the world around you with spiritual guidance. The Armor of God bolsters your discernment. Paul says in Ephesians that we first must put on the belt of truth before we can put on any other part of the armor. Truth is what everything else is predicated on.

The Latin phrase *sola scriptura*, meaning scripture alone, theologically points out that all of scripture is God-breathed, and God's Word alone is sufficient. [2 Timothy 3:16] Therefore we must accept *all* of the Bible as truth with a capital "T." We don't throw out what we don't like and only keep what we like from scripture. We must keep everything in it, even the Truths that make us uncomfortable. Therefore, when it comes time for us to defend the Truth, either to ourselves or someone else, we have an unshakable foundation that is solidified through Jesus Christ and not ourselves. People are not the arbiters of Truth, like some may suggest on social media. God is.

So, how do we decipher what is Truth? The only way we can be sure of the Truth is to saturate ourselves in it, so we can recognize it or discern when something is not biblically true. Back in Jesus's day, the Pharisees and Sadducees were more preoccupied with proving that Jesus wasn't the Messiah than trying to discern what was right in front of them. Jesus says, "Blessed are those who have not seen and yet believe." [John 20:29] That is us! We did not live in Jesus's day or see the miracles that he performed, but the religious leaders of the time did.

Jesus performed miracle after miracle in front of their very eyes, but they still asked him to show more signs from heaven to prove He was the Son of God. In their unbelief Jesus replied, "When evening comes, you say, 'It will be good weather because the sky is red.' And in the morning, 'Today will be stormy because the sky is red and threatening.' You know how to read the appearance of the sky, but you can't read the signs of the times." [Matthew 16: 2–3] Jesus was pointing out the high priests were able to see the weather coming, yet were unable to recognize the Son of God performing miracles right in front of their eyes. Not much has changed in two thousand years, has it?! We too can look up at the sky and discern the impending weather better than we can discern the truths and lies of the modern era.

Back then, the Truth was the Messiah, in their presence. Today, Truth at its foundation is fully accepting the Messiah into our hearts in an unshakable, life-changing, chain-breaking way that allows us to conquer things like our bad habits on social media. All other biblical truths stem from Jesus.

Right after Jesus's enemies were condemned for not using discernment, Christ's own followers in Matthew 16 were guilty of forgetting the Truth right in front of them, too. To paint a picture: The disciples were complaining amongst themselves about the lack of bread. Keep in mind, this was after they had seen Jesus feed five thousand people with five loaves of bread and two fish, and perform miracles involving food, water, and wine. Jesus had never let them go hungry, why would he now? Jesus reminds them of those miracles and drives his point home:

"How is it that you don't understand that when I told you, 'Beware of the leaven of the Pharisees and Sadducees,' it wasn't about bread? Then [the disciples] understood that he had not told them to beware of the leaven in bread, but of the teaching of the Pharisees and the Sadducees."
—Matthew 16: 11–12

Even the disciples had to be reminded that Jesus, the living bread [John 6:51], is Truth [John 14:6]. The Truth of Jesus was the only nourishment they needed, and even his most beloved and original disciples forgot the Truth while he was with them. If Jesus's chosen twelve disciples had to be reminded to avoid false teaching and lies, then we, also a part of God's chosen followers [Matthew 22:14, John 15:16], who spend less time in church and in the Word and more time in front of screens than any generation before us, most certainly have to be reminded of that daily. In order to discern the Truth for ourselves and share it with others, we must be inspired to put in the time educating ourselves about the Bible and its teachings.

Wherever the Truth is, God is.

> "If God is for us, who is against us?"
> —Romans 8:31

Even if you share or live by Truth that upsets someone, God is on your side. You do not answer to that offended person or to society; if you are a follower of Jesus Christ, you ultimately answer to Him. Jesus tells us directly that, "on the day of judgment, people will have to account for every careless word they speak. For by your words you will be acquitted, and by your words you will be condemned." [Matthew 12: 36–37]

That sounds harsh, doesn't it? Don't get me wrong, Jesus was loving, but he didn't play around with the Truth. If the Bible says our words will be condemned, and that we will be held accountable for accepting or denying the Truth on the day of judgment, who will we be answering to? The answer is great news! And it's found right there in the book of Truth.

> "Who can bring an accusation against God's elect? God is the one
> who justifies. Who is the one who condemns? Christ Jesus is the one
> who died, but even more, has been raised; he also is at the right hand
> of God and intercedes for us."
> —Romans 8: 33-34

Jesus is the one who intercedes for us. He is our advocate. He knows our hearts and will step in on our day of judgment to vouch for where our hearts lie. Even if we don't always get the Truth right, he will know where our true intentions lie. He knows how we regard the Holy Truth and he is our only way to God the Father. We've seen how the enemy's oldest trick is to twist the truth, and now social media is a place he's added to his spiritual battle ground. But no matter if we have bought into some of Satan's lies or not on social media, God knows where our hearts lie in the end. And He's equipped us with the belt of truth to measure our thoughts and actions to scripture.

Given how Satan operates, it's no surprise that content that generates the most likes on social media, more often than not, isn't posts about charity, service, or humility. Those don't promote his anti-God agenda. The posts that usually receive the most attention are suggestive, sexually provocative, and/or self-promotional.

Of course, no one wants to post unflattering photos of themselves for the public to see, but when we take it further than that, idolizing how we look, obsessing over our appearance, or posing or dancing in such a way to encourage others to lust over us, we are fishing to get man's approval, not God's. Today's youth, and even adults, have been swept up in the "Instagram model" culture. Posting photos of themselves, obsessing over how they look and hoping others take notice. Some take it a step further, showing off their bodies, cleavage, and more for all to see. Tiktok is another platform that promotes accounts that post explicit videos of themselves dancing in hopes of gaining eyeballs on their content.

God's Word shares with us the truth about how posts like this may have a domino effect on ourselves and those around us. In biblical times, the punishment for breaking the seventh commandment, "Thou shall not commit adultery" [Exodus 20:1–4] was death. The historical account in the Gospels describes the Pharisees catching a woman in the act of adultery, dragging her to the temple, and presenting her before Jesus, then reminding him that she should be stoned according to the law. However, Jesus prompted the Pharisees to look beyond the act itself. Jesus pointed to what's in our hearts as even more important than just simply following rules.

> "But I say to you that everyone who looks at a woman with lustful intent has already committed adultery with her in his heart."
> —Matthew 5:28

The harsh reality is that a girl who posts a suggestive photo or video is seducing someone else to sin. She is inciting other men to commit adultery in their hearts as they scroll through their phones. So not only is she inviting others to do something they know deep down is wrong, she's tearing down her own house before she's even had a chance to build it.

> "The wise woman builds her house, but with her own hands, the foolish one tears hers down."
> —Proverbs 14:1

Social media is encouraging young girls to compromise their dignity before they're even close to thinking about marriage, family, or the proverbial home they'd someday like to build, when that time comes. Breaking it down this way certainly isn't popular, but if we don't come face-to-face with the lies social media can feed us, how do we overcome them? How do we develop our discernment and choose righteousness if we don't know what is right—or accept what is wrong?

The way youth are influenced to present themselves online opens the door to that activity snowballing. Sixty-five percent of teens in America have shared a nude image with someone else or have looked at one.[6] Much of this takes place via coercion in private messaging, according to Jaco Booyens Ministry, who rescues people from sex trafficking. Their ministry is sounding the alarm on pornography's devastating effects on the United States and worldwide. The prevalence of social media's role in the corruption of young people is well beyond what most realize.

The average age of a child's first exposure to pornography in the United States is eight to ten years old.[7] Additionally, according to Booyens, their first exposure is likely to be viewing a sexual encounter featuring at least three people—a far cry from the adult magazines from a decade or two prior that served as some young people's first introduction, which were covered up or located in a private section of select stores. All of this is a harsh reality to face. The fast track to corruption can start with how we present ourselves online and what we allow others to convince us to do in "private messages." This makes discernment, studying, and learning Truths like biblical modesty and righteousness all the more important in today's online climate. Establishing or rebuilding a Faith Filter on a foundation of a biblical worldview is essential. The Armor of God protects us as we step out with our biblical foundation.

The second piece in the Armor of God one puts on after the belt of truth is the breastplate of righteousness. Despite being a warrior for the Lord, these were two valuable pieces of the Armor of God David bypassed later in his life that we can learn from in light of sexual sin and the heartbreak that can ensue. King David had a special place in God's heart, and that is because of the love David had for the Lord. God loved David so much that he established Christ's bloodline through David. But David, just like us, was far from perfect.

David was a very successful ruler on the battlefield. God was with David and delivered his enemies into David's hands time-after-time. After years of success in war, which led to his people hailing him as a great king, David became lazy. He sent his commanders to defend Israel in his place. One day, while his armies were fending off Israel's enemies, David wandered the palace and saw a beautiful woman bathing, so he sent one of his servants to find out who it was. Her name was Bathsheba, and she was the wife of one of his commanders that he had ushered off to war in his absence, but David sent for her and slept with her anyway.

His lust and his wandering eyes led to the physical act of adultery, which, remember, was an act punishable by death. How did David come to see her? Was she bathing in sight of others or putting herself in a position for wandering eyes to see her? Was she coerced into sin? Or a tragic victim? Perhaps it was one or all of these. In no way do we want to belittle circumstances even remotely close to these that anyone today has gone through, and we do not want to point blame to any victims of abuse, but instead we want to extend mercy and comfort to all.

The Bible doesn't make Bathsheba's circumstances clear. However, what is clear is that her house was torn down. King David went on to arrange for the murder of her husband. This was an attempt for David to cover his tracks after he found out Bathsheba was pregnant with his baby. Both David and Bathsheba suffered greatly. Their circumstances led to tragedy and death.

Yet, if we have love for Him in our hearts, our gracious God redeems us. Bathsheba went on to give birth to David's son Solomon, who would build God's glorious temple in more ways than one. King Solomon erected God's earthly dwelling place in Jerusalem *and* carried on the bloodline that would eventually lead to Jesus. In fact, his mother, Bathsheba, is one of just five women listed in Jesus's genealogy in Matthew 1. Our transgressions are never too big for God to forgive. Our tragedies are never too great to overcome with His help. Satan tries to defeat us, but Christ always wins.

The Lord has given us the sword of the Spirit, which is the word of God, [Ephesians 6:17] to learn from the stories the Bible provides. So, despite the pressures of society, Hollywood, and social media, modesty is what women and all of us are called to practice. Additionally, you don't have to be pressured into sharing private photos you are uncomfortable with or coerced to sin. Jesus can break any and all shackles bonding you to sin. He can forgive and release you from any tragic circumstances so you will not carry that burden on your own anymore.

When the Pharisees so eagerly brought the adulterous woman to Jesus, he spoke directly to her, offering his forgiveness:

> "Neither do I condemn you; go and from now on sin no more."
> —Luke 8:11

Because of society's normalization of everyone's need for attention and putting ourselves out there, many don't even realize what they are doing is sinful or are not aware of the tragedies that could later take place in private messages. That environment unfortunately has led to people "sliding into your DMs," a regular occurrence for anyone to encounter online. For women, that can include men contacting you via private messages telling you how pretty you are, asking you out, even requesting private photos or videos of you, or sending unsolicited graphic content of their own. So, if you are practicing modesty and do get these messages of pursuit, how do you follow up? What do you allow to take place next?

I want to emphasize, any abuse that anyone endures, no matter the circumstances, is tragic and no blame is being made. Christ conquers all and we can find healing through his comfort and eternal gift of salvation. But these are very real issues that are important for social media consumers, especially young girls, to reflect on and discuss. If this discussion saves anyone from having to endure a tragic situation in the future or points someone to Christ to help them if they have already gone through a similar tragedy, it is worth it.

My future husband began his pursuit of me with respect and after a life-long friendship. How are others pursuing you? Is it with respect? How do you respond to their pursuit? If they are not approaching you with respect, or you don't feel comfortable, never, under any circumstances are you required to respond or to keep anything uncomfortable a secret. Confide in the Lord and a person of trust to help you.

David wrote Psalm 51 as a lament of remorse, asking for God's mercy and recognizing God's love and forgiveness as the ways through his transgressions. David's story also shows us that when we have extra time and don't use it wisely, it can lead to sin. The third piece in the Armor of God, "shoes for your feet, having put on the readiness given by the gospel of peace," [Ephesians 6:15] implies by using the word "readiness" that we should always be alert and ready to share the gospel at all times. Vigilance is achieved by putting in time in the Word and being productive, not idle. So many of us find ourselves lost in our phones, scrolling through social media, only to have lost out on valuable time in our day. We must use discernment to know when we've spent enough time on social media and need to move on to more productive things.

In this arena, the devil has traded a truth for a lie by calling productivity "adulting" and attaching a negative connotation to service. Things that God calls for us to do that involve taking care of our homes, families, paying bills, doing schoolwork, etc., today's world has led us to believe are burdens. But those aren't burdens, those are what we are supposed to be doing! Yes, getting your nails done, playing video games, or binge-watching the latest television drama all sound like a lot more fun. And when done in moderation, they can be fruits of our labor, but we must labor first! In a world that rewards idleness, the Bible warns us against it. According to Proverbs 31, one of the many virtues of a prosperous woman is productivity:

"She looks well to the ways of her household,
And does not eat the bread of idleness."
—Proverbs 31:27

After the Shield of Faith, the Helmet of Salvation, and the Sword of the Spirit, prayer is the final piece of the Armor of God. Use social media to reach out to someone to ask how you could pray for them. Flip over to your Bible App or your memory verse screen saver that will be outlined in Chapter 8. Put your device down with enough time to talk to God directly through a little prayer in your spare moments. Prayer can prevent idleness from snowballing into other sinful activities, especially if you pray for God to work on building up the fruits of the Spirit in your daily actions.

"At the same time, they also learn to be idle, going from house to
house; they are not only idle, but are also gossips and busybodies,
saying things they shouldn't say."
—1 Timothy 5:13

Perhaps consuming negative news or emotionally charged content centered around social issues, politics, etc., has gotten you so worked up that you've said something you shouldn't say online in comments or private messages. Consuming too much negative news content is also a battle many face online. The Shield of Faith will help you "extinguish all the flaming darts of the evil one," [Ephesians 6:16] while the Helmet of Salvation reminds you of what is important in terms of eternity versus the things that are passing away.

No matter what situation you find yourself in on social media, the Armor of God can deliver you. And your Faith Filter will grow stronger as you work to build up your discernment through taking part in things like small groups, where you'll not only study the Bible with other believers, but you will build life-on-life relationships that will help you grow as a person and a Christian, well beyond what social media can do. Then you will be even more ready to take part in social media, dressed as a member of the Lord's Army.

Chapter 7 Devotional

1. Building on Chapter 6's Tracking Challenge: How much time this past week did you spend in the Word and with Jesus? _____ vs. on your device _____ ? (See page 86 to see how to find that information in your phone.)

2. Read Ephesians 6:10–20 and list each piece in the Armor of God. Next to it, write how each piece of armor can help you personally with your social media activity:

Armor of God	How it can help you on social media
(v. 14) _____ of _____ =	
(v. 14) _____ of _____ =	
(v. 15) Shoes for your feet fitted with _____ =	
(v. 16) _____ of _____ =	
(v. 17) _____ of _____ =	
(v. 17) _____ of the _____ =	
(v. 18) Pray in the Spirit on all occasions =	

3. How does knowing you have the Armor of God to apply to your social media activity encourage you to continue working on any struggles you may have on social media or with your device usage?

4. Read more verses about discernment, which are listed below. Write out the full texts of the verses that impacted you the most on a separate piece of paper:
   - Ephesians 5:10
   - Proverbs 14:8
   - Isaiah 44:18
   - 1 Kings 3:9–14
   - Romans 12:2
   - Hebrews 5:14

5. Given these verses, how important is discernment for a Christian? How can you work on growing your discernment this week?

Soul Influence Challenge

6. Have you taken part in posting photos or videos that may have prompted others to lust after you? Or ventured down the wrong path in private messages? Or know someone else who has been struggling in this arena?

   • Pause and take their name or your struggles to the Lord in prayer.

7. Next, give yourself grace and take up the Sword of the Spirit (the word of God) and see how others in similar situations in the Bible have been forgiven:

   • A Sinful Woman Forgiven [Luke 7:36–50]
   • Jesus Forgives the Woman at the Well [John 4:1–42]
   • God Uses Rahab To Help Israel [Joshua 2] And Appears in Jesus's Genealogy [Matthew 1:5]

Prayer

Dear Lord,

Thank you for searching my heart. You are acquainted with all my ways and discern my thoughts and actions from afar. I praise you, for I am fearfully and wonderfully made. Even in the depths of my actions, your hand leads me and your right hand holds me. You formed, ahead of time, all my days with a purpose and as a means to sharpen me. So now I come before you, praying that you will search my heart and show me any grievous way in me, and lead me in the way everlasting! I pray that you will equip me with discernment and show me how to use the Armor of God to cultivate it.

Amen.

(Note: This prayer was adapted from Psalm 139. I encourage you to look it up!)

Chapter 8

Surrender

Surrender. Society usually associates that word with defeat. If you are fighting a battle, it's the losing side that surrenders. But if you are going through a tough season, you might want nothing more than to surrender—to end the battle and be done. In that instance, surrender could bring on thoughts of relief and feel like a miracle.

What if you were to surrender everything to the Ultimate Influencer? What comes to mind then? Relief, peace, comfort, salvation?

So many of us have surrendered our time to our devices, our sense of self-worth to our social media pages, our ideals to the ones who influence us, and our identities to our profiles or political affiliations. We spend all of our time looking down at our devices, instead of looking up to Jesus. What if we surrendered all that and rendered it miniscule in light of the One that died on the cross for us? How would that change how you handle social media? Jesus Christ wants *all* of you, not just certain parts. He wants the good, the bad, and everything in between. How much of your life have you surrendered to Him? All of it? Some of it? Only a little of it? Is social media one of the last pieces you are holding on to?

Sometimes God pushes us to surrender when we are still gripping tightly. It's by His mercy that He nudges us in the right direction. Like when you've been wanting to kick that habit of devouring Flamin' Hot Cheetos and one day, the grocery store is out. (Thank you, Lord! I couldn't have done it without you.) Or when you've been trying to cut back on social media consumption, and you still find yourself sucked into the scroll more than you'd like. Yet, one day, Instagram is experiencing a technical issue, and the app keeps crashing on you, so you aren't able to view anything on it all day. (Thank you, Jesus! I needed that forced break!)

Then there are a few big moments throughout our lives that make it unmistakable we couldn't do anything without Him. I've had my fair share of them. For example, I had no choice but to surrender all control when CBSSports.com came calling. It came out of nowhere, I wasn't looking for a new job, I was busy trying to expand my role as the St. Louis Cardinals Multimedia Reporter.

When I was offered to make the jump to CBS Sports, on the surface, many would think it would be a no-brainer to take the fabulous opportunity. But I admit, it was a huge leap of faith for me—a big step out of my comfort zone. I was in a job I enjoyed, working for a team I loved, in the city I grew up in, surrounded by friends, family, and a sweet boyfriend. All the while, I was grateful for the sudden opportunity.

In fact, it was so sudden, I had to make the decision in less than two days. If I accepted, I had to then move across the country in a week and a half. (Good thing I still lived in my parents' basement! I didn't have too much to pack.) But it was hard for me to leave my boyfriend and an entire group of friends I had grown up with since preschool. Sometimes amazing opportunities, no matter how big of a blessing, can be scary and nerve wracking, unless we surrender it all to God.

"Yes" was my final answer in a day and a half. Jesus took the wheel at that point because it sure was clear I wasn't the one driving this ship! I dropped everything to move my life 1,500 miles to a job that didn't end up being exactly what I thought it would be, in a town I didn't fall in love with. There wasn't any instant gratification. They didn't give me football and basketball sideline reporting opportunities like they had promised. Plus, this Midwestern girl didn't feel at home in Fort Lauderdale, FL, which was much like its neighboring Miami. To top it all off, my apartment was infested with cockroaches (like antennas sticking out of my light switches, infested). No joke! They lived under my oven, sometimes crawled above my head at night while I was in bed. It still gives me nightmares just thinking about it.

But what I was too distracted to realize was that God was at work in bigger ways than I realized. And it was all possible because I had surrendered everything to Him. This opportunity wasn't at all what I had hoped for when I said, "yes," but something (or Someone) told me it was all going to be ok. It was by His grace that I was sent to South Florida, the heart of minor league golf in that part of the country.

My boyfriend from the Midwest started playing golf professionally on the Florida minor league tours and was able to travel down to spend long periods of time with me while pursuing his own career. The career move to CBSSports.com also gave me the chance to cover PGA TOUR golf for the first time—a niche I settled into nicely with my passion for the game. God opened doors for me after nearly a year of not feeling at home and like a fish out of water. I landed a job with the PGA TOUR and moved to North Florida where the people there made it feel more like the Midwest (except at the beach.) My boyfriend proposed, became my husband, and we started a family.

By surrendering it all, I gained it all because of God's grace.

Maybe your way of surrendering to His will isn't a spontaneous move across the country. Maybe it's how you've reframed the community you follow on social media or how you post on it. Or how you've finally been able to limit your time on social media by logging off ten minutes before you normally would to read a bible devotional.

Lately, surrendering looks different for me, too. Now, making decisions for our family comes after a lot of time in prayer, so we trust they are a part of His plan. Even when it's hard, we trust. Trusting in God above ourselves gives my husband and I a peaceful feeling, resulting in less anxiety than what we see in society around us. Our past and recent experiences have shown us that the Holy Spirit is with us. We're starting to understand that the little things don't matter nearly as much as eternity. We live for Him and trust that He is equipping us to arm our family with biblical truth and that He is leading our steps. In so many ways we have a peace that surpasses understanding, while at the same time we see the areas where we need to surrender more to gain more peace. In no way are we perfect in this arena, but we are making conscious efforts to improve our faith.

How much do you trust God? We can all learn from examples like Abraham, who trusted his son's life to the Lord when God asked Abraham to do the unthinkable. God tested Abraham to prove that Abraham's faith and trust far surpassed what he realized. Abraham obeyed God's command and took his heir Isaac up the mountain to surrender his son as a lamb to God. Just as Abraham was about to sacrifice his son, an angel of the Lord called out to him, "Abraham; Abraham!" [Genesis 22:11] And Abraham replied:

> "'Here I am.' Then [the angel] said, 'Do not lay your hand on the boy or do anything to him. For now, I know that you fear God, since you have not withheld your only son from me.'"
> —Genesis 22: 11–13

"Here I am."

I want you to imagine saying those words of Abraham to God right now.

"Here I am surrendering it all to You."

Right after the angel of the Lord stopped Abraham from sacrificing Isaac on the altar, a ram appeared close by. Abraham took that ram and sacrificed it on the altar instead, a foreshadow of how God would make a substitutional sacrifice on the cross for us through His Son Jesus. Abraham named that spot on the mountain where this incredible leap of faith took place, "The Lord Will Provide." [Genesis 22:14] And isn't that the truth?! He may not provide in the way you had planned in your head because His ways are not our ways, and His thoughts are not our thoughts. [Isaiah 55:8]

Sometimes surrender doesn't look as noble as Abraham. Sometimes it comes after much internal struggle, like Abraham's wife Sarah experienced. God told Abraham and Sarah that He would give them a child, despite their old age and the fact that Sarah was barren. After a while had passed and still no baby like God had promised, Sarah took things into her own hands and gave Abraham her slave, Hagar, to conceive an heir. Hagar bore Ishmael and what followed was a story of jealousy and heartbreak for both women. Despite all that, God still provided Sarah with her son Isaac.

Surrender can be difficult when we let our inner voice of doubt and fear, which are messages from the enemy, take over. Surrender can also be difficult if we let the loud voices around us drown out our calls from God. David knew God would deliver when all he had was a sling and a rock. Young David, with his casual, angelic demeanor, trusted God was on his side and that with God's help he could slay a giant. In order to do so, David had to ignore the loud voices of the cheering armies, the giant, and his own people around him, and focus only on God.

When David first showed up to the army's camp, his older brother chastised him for leaving their flock. Then King Saul told him there's no way he would defeat the giant Philistine as just a small boy. But David, who had fended off wild animals while tending his sheep, had the perfect answer.

> "The Lord who rescued me from the paw of the lion and the paw of the bear will rescue me from the hand of this Philistine." —1 Samuel 17:37

Before his heroic deed, David had another voice to ignore—the taunts of the giant himself, who boasted with pride before he was humbled forever.

Elite athletes are modern examples of people who need to be able to drown out all the noise from the fans and the game around them to execute. I imagine David was in the zone like that. He didn't listen to all the loud noises around him. He trusted God and surrendered himself to the moment. I would also imagine that act brought him closer to God than he had ever been before.

We battle the noises around us daily. The media, those we follow, the news we take in—there are so many voices it seems impossible to drown them out these days. Not to mention the voices of doubt we may hear in our own heads from the devil himself, on top of it all. Are you able to drown it all out like David did? Can you take it a step further and bring yourself closer to God in the process by surrendering your trust to Him? That seems like a big ask, doesn't it? Everything you do should have that end goal.

So, how can social media bring us closer to God? David's goal was to be closer to God, so was Abraham's, and (in her roundabout way) so was Sarah's. We all have that desire.

When I surrendered my social media account to Christ and began sharing the gospel and truth, everything changed for me. Although I still struggle to drown out the noise, it's a lot easier these days because I no longer care about how many likes I get, how many followers I have, how pretty my picture is. I only care that people get a small glimpse of His glory. If I can help just one person see His saving grace and the truth, it's all worth it. That's all that matters. I started posting for Him; not for me.

I started posting about my faith at the height of my career, while I was a broadcaster for the PGA TOUR. My social media following dropped. I no longer have the same number of people following me. My posts no longer get the same number of likes—but they are changing lives. I can't take credit for any of it, it's all orchestrated by Him. God is doing the work in their hearts. A piece of content may say one thing to me, but then I hear from a follower how it went to work differently in their heart. That's the power of the Holy Spirit, and it's so much greater than empty likes.

Social media was one of the final pieces for me. My zeal for Jesus jumped to another level. By sharing my faith on social media, I surrendered. I walked away from the societal pressure to be a picture-perfect broadcaster online. By surrendering, I found relief. One day, I shared a Bible verse in my post, then I did it again and again. I just kept sharing what God was sharing with me. I started unfollowing people that were posting toxic materialism, hatred, and false ideologies —and started following more accounts sharing the gospel. By breaking free of the bondage of social media, I surrendered a large part of my identity to Christ. My faith walk took a giant leap forward. A part of my old self died and a part of me was made new. [Colossians 3:3] With God's help, I took a leap of surrendering my social media activity, and now I know I can do it in other parts of my life. I am overjoyed by the fruit I know it can produce. You can do it, too. Just try sharing the gospel with someone one time and you'll be empowered to do it again.

We can take heart knowing that we are taking steps toward righteousness when our wants start to align with God's. Social media keeps us sucked into the desires of the masses. Through it, we let society frame our appetites. When we receive what we desire, we only achieve temporary happiness. When we yearn for what God wants, we experience eternal joy. Are you letting social media frame your longings? Is what you are consuming preventing you from wanting what God wants? I invite you to surrender your social media to Him. Apply the Faith Filter to everything: who you follow, what you post, what you read. Use social media as a tool to point you to God; to help fill up your cup, not drain it.

Now I follow primarily Christian accounts and post mostly about Christ, the Good News, truth, and how my family is doing our best to live out our faith. It has made all the difference for me, and I know it can for you, too. Even when I am looking down at my phone, I'm still looking up to Him. And he, being the Ultimate Influencer, is the highest earthly example of what it looks like to surrender. Jesus, walking in our shoes here on earth, knew what it was like to be tempted and knew what it was like to have to give himself up in the most horrific circumstances. And he surrendered it all for you.

> "For we do not have a high priest who is unable to sympathize
> with our weaknesses, but one who in every respect has
> been tempted as we are, yet without sin."
> —Hebrews 4:15

Jesus sees you and knows what it's like to be hungry for Earthly temptations. He understands your temptations to allow distractions and social media to take over your thoughts and time. Two instances are recorded in scripture of Jesus's temptation. Note that both tales of temptation come just after a high point in Jesus's earthly life.

In the first temptation account, Jesus retreats to the desert to fast for forty days after his baptism in the Jordan River, where Satan meets him with hopes to tempt him. In his efforts, Satan told Jesus if he was truly the Son of God and hungry from a forty-day fast, he should command the stones to become bread. But Jesus knew that we are not fueled by earthly pleasures.

> "Man shall not live by bread alone." —Luke 4:4

As that episode continues, Satan tried again in the desert, showing Jesus all the glorious kingdoms he could rule alone. But Jesus knew that there is only One that deserves our worship, time, and adoration.

> "You shall worship the Lord your God, and him only shall you serve."
> —Luke 4:8

Jesus had two choices of surrender in the desert: God or temptation —just as we do each time we find ourselves scrolling on our phones for too long; just as we do each seductive photo we are tempted to post; just as we do each time we are reading our Bible app and see a new email alert pop up on our device. Next time you can pause and intentionally choose to limit your time on media for a chance to be in the Word, in prayer, or working to glorify His kingdom.

After Jesus resisted Satan in the desert, scripture says:

> "And when the devil had ended every temptation, he departed from him until an opportune time."
> —Luke 4:13

Temptation will return.

Jesus also felt tempted by his flesh after the Last Supper—a bitter-sweet and iconic moment in Christian history. After that final meal with his beloved followers, he went to the Garden of Gethsemane with a few of the disciples and warned Peter, "Watch and pray that you may not enter into temptation." [Matthew 26:41] Instead of praying, Peter and the other two disciples fell asleep, leaving Jesus alone in his battle with his flesh. In that battle, Jesus asked God to let the cup of his upcoming crucifixion and ultimate act of surrender, to pass from him. [Matthew 26:39 & 42]

These points in Jesus's earthly life show us that we too will be tempted in or after prominent or joyous moments. So, when you feel like you are dominating resistance to temptations and that you have gotten yourself to a great place of limiting social media use and pouring more time into your walk with the Lord, you are at your most vulnerable. You are in a place to more easily slip up because you are riding on the high. Your mind has forgotten about what it's like to be down.

However, now, you are equipped to recognize it. And thanks to the Ultimate Influencer, you are shown how to quickly and easily deflect those temptations—surrender. Surrender to the King of Grace, rather than the disguised prince of darkness. Just after Hebrews 4:15 tells us that Jesus is able to sympathize with our weaknesses because he was tempted just as we are, scripture invites us to surrender our temptations.

> "Let us then with confidence draw near to the throne of grace, that we may receive mercy and find grace to help in time of need."
> —Hebrews 4:16

Surrender your temptations to the One who loves you, to the One who sympathizes with your weaknesses, to the One that forgives you and will deliver you—not the one who takes pleasure as you wallow in your vices. If you need a reminder of who to turn to in times of temptation, memorize this verse to have it in your arsenal in a time of need.

"I will greatly rejoice in the Lord; my soul shall exult in my God, for he has clothed me with the garments of salvation, he has covered me with the robe of righteousness, as a bridegroom decks himself like a priest with a beautiful headdress, and as a bride adorns herself with her jewels."
—Isaiah 61:10

Whether it's beautiful verses like this, scripture full of wisdom, theological concepts, intimate details about God, or examples from stories of people in the Bible, we are urged to study scripture, memorize it, and live by it. The Bible tells us to store up God's Word in our hearts, so that we might not sin against Him. [Psalm 119:11]

Using your favorite Bible App, create a memory verse screen saver. Screenshot a verse or series of verses you'd like to memorize for the week. Set it as your screen saver and challenge yourself to memorize it. Read it *before* opening up social media, messages, or email. Then cut your time on those outlets short to go back to working on your memory verse again afterward. Let it sink in and teach yourself of various scriptures diligently, "when you sit in your house, and when you walk by the way, and when you lie down, and when you rise." [Deuteronomy 6:7] And it will help you to continue to surrender your device to the Lord.

Chapter 8 Devotional

1. In what ways are you currently relying only on yourself?

2. What can you give over to Jesus right now?

3. What is something you've done recently you are proud of?

4. Tangibly, how did Jesus literally help you make that happen?

5. Jesus Christ wants *all* of you, not just certain parts. He wants the good, the bad, and everything in between. How much of your life have you surrendered to Him? All of it? Some of it? Only a little of it?

6. Is social media one of the pieces you are holding on to?

SOUL INFLUENCE CHALLENGE

7. There are many others who have answered, "Here I am",
   like Abraham, throughout the Bible.
   - Read 1 Samuel 3:1–21, then fill in the blanks from
     scripture:
     - (v. 7) "Now Samuel did _____ yet _____
       the Lord."
     - But as you'll read in verses (4, 5, 6 & 8) he still
       answered God's call with "_____."
       Count how many times he answered God's call
       with "Here I am": _____ number of times.
     - What did God do for Samuel as a result of him
       answering His call? (v. 19 & 20)

8. List others who have answered God with "Here I am":
   - Genesis 22:1
   - Genesis 31:11
   - Exodus 3:4
   - Isaiah 6:8
   - Acts 9:10

9. God provides for us when we surrender ourselves to Him. What is one way you can say, "Here I am" to Him today?

10. Sarah was an example of someone who forced their will, and she did so through her servant Hagar. What did Hagar, after her sufferings through Sarah, name her baby? (Genesis 16:11)

11. In Hebrew, Ishmael means "God hears." God always hears you, no matter what you are going through. Are you hearing Him? What is He saying to you lately?

12. Are there ways you are allowing too much noise to creep in, preventing you from hearing God clearly?

Prayer

Ask the Lord to drown out all the other noise, so you can focus on Him:

Here I am, Lord. Please allow me to focus on your will for my life. Help me to drown out the societal noise around me. Help me to look past myself and my screen and up to you. Help me to realize you do hear me; you are the God who hears. You know my deepest dilemmas, you know my greatest triumphs, even the ones I have not yet experienced. I know none of them will happen if I don't focus and do everything for you. Please keep YOU at the forefront of my thoughts, words and social media use. Help me surrender it all to you, because even that act of surrender cannot be done without you.

Amen.

CHAPTER 9
Sacrifice

After surrendering himself to the Roman soldiers, through Judas's kiss of betrayal, Jesus became our sacrificial lamb. What once was a perfect gift on the altar in Jewish custom, a spotless lamb, was now a nation's living sacrifice.

Traditionally, a spotless lamb was born and raised with the utmost care. Special flocks were raised by the Jewish priesthood. When the time came, the mother lambs were brought into specific ritually pure and anointed caves where they would give birth. Those lambs would then be swaddled in cloth, to ensure they did not get a single spot or bump on them, as they wandered clumsily about the ceremonious cave in their first few days of life. These sacrificial lambs had to remain unblemished to be fit for offering.

Some biblical scholars trace Jesus's birth back to one of these caves—not the dusty stable we set up in the manger scene each Christmas, but a dark, clean, purified birth cave, where spotless lambs were brought into this world to become living sacrifices. It's a fitting and symbolic entrance for our spotless (void of sin) sacrificial lamb, Jesus, to be born in the very place, where traditional sacrificial lambs had been for generations prior. Only this time our lamb would not be carefully and ceremoniously offered up to God.

Instead, they gruesomely made a sport of his death: whipping him, marching him through the streets, forcing him to carry the weight of the cross, blood dripping from his wounds, a crown of thorns mockingly placed on his head, all while his mother watched.

At the end of the road of misery, he was then forced to climb the hill at Calvary. Nails driven into his hands, one-by-one, hammered, blow-by-blow, into the wood of the cross. The physical torture is more than any of us could bear, but the spiritual battle he fought for us is beyond reproach. Jesus absorbed *all* of our sin that day, taking on everything in your life that has been too hard to battle or too hard to carry. He did that for you, me, and every single one of us throughout time. The Son of Man, who lived a perfect life, never doing anything wrong, took on all the sin of his followers combined in the hours he hung there.

"God made him who had no sin to be sin for us,
so that in him we might become the righteousness of God."
—2 Corinthians 5:21 ESV

We don't usually contemplate the enormity of what Jesus absorbed, even at times like Easter, when we are studying it together as a church, likely because we cannot and will not ever fully understand what our awesome Savior did for us, his followers, while we inhabit this earth. The magnitude is just too enormous. But that's what Jesus was referring to when he said, "It is finished." [John 19:30]

If the Son of God had to surrender and give the ultimate sacrifice, we have to assume that we will also have to make sacrifices of our own, too. Jesus says so in scripture when he states, "a servant is not greater than his master, nor a messenger greater than the one who sent him," [John 13:16] which indicated to his disciples, who he is speaking to in this passage, that they should not expect better treatment than him. If you follow him, you will endure much of the same trials. We've already talked about the sacrifice Abraham was willing to make, handing over the life of his son Isaac, who God rescued from the altar due to Abraham's faith, as well as several other followers of God who were willing to lay what they held most dear on the line for the Lord. Therefore, we'll have to, too.

Although no sacrifice is easy, if you have already surrendered yourself over to following him, you may have a great feeling of peace when it's time for you to take up your cross, regardless of how it affects your social media standing or any other areas of your life. If you've made it this far, if you've already given your life to Christ and are living for eternity and not worldly ideas, the possible suffering of your sacrifice will feel like the only path you can take. This is a payment worth making and a battle worth fighting—willingly and, dare I say, even with traces of gratitude. And it likely won't be just once, but I imagine with each subsequent sacrifice, you'll be even more ready, more equipped, and more at peace.

Sometimes sacrifices are small or incremental. You are called daily to pick up your cross. [Luke 9:23] And we do so by living our lives for God, through the service of others and standing firm on the gospel. Maybe you are called today to pick up your cross by being a good and caring friend; or you have to lay yourself aside in your daily duties as a parent to care for your children or as someone who is a caretaker to an elderly, sick, or disabled loved one; or you are called to stand firm on the Bible when faced with someone opposing Christ; or put yourself and faith out there with someone in need of hearing the gospel.

Other sacrifices are much bigger, and often happen during pivotal moments in your life where making a sacrifice alters the course of your path permanently. But the grace and mercy of God is so great that the worst moments in your life also teach the greatest lessons.

All of us were impacted by COVID-19. It will leave an imprint on us all for the rest of our lives. For me, it became a moment where I had to stand firm in my faith publicly and privately, not allowing the world to sway me in the way that I knew was wrong for my family. By coming out on the other side and surviving the trial, it taught me that I am able to wade through pivotal sacrificial times personally. I now *know* I can survive times of great sacrifice and won't hesitate to make those difficult leaps for my faith again. I relied on discernment to wade through the inconsistencies, my biblical knowledge of the sanctity of life to do what was best for my unborn child, and peace that surpasses all understanding to know that my Lord and Savior had me in the palm of his hand through it all. [Philippians 4:7]

After months of sleepless nights battling with my employer, in November 2021 the PGA TOUR fired me, while I was pregnant with our second child, concluding nearly six years of reporting for them and a lifetime of pouring everything into my sports broadcasting career. It all ended, publicly, on social media, over something that had nothing to do with my job performance and everything to do with my faith. No matter where you stand on the COVID-19 injection mandates and the policies that surround them, you likely know someone that was impacted. In no way am I a martyr, or braver than anyone else; I'm just a mom. And you, too, can stand strong for what you believe in, whether on social media, in school, in the workplace, or in a public square.

> "If they persecuted me, they will also persecute you."
> —John 15:20

Just as Jesus warned us that we, too, will be persecuted, remember what he also said to us in that eighth beatitude in his Sermon on the Mount?

> "Blessed are those who are persecuted for righteousness' sake, for theirs is the kingdom of heaven."
> —Matthew 5:10

At this juncture, sacrifice for me came in the form of laying it all on the line and standing firm in my faith. Though your call to stand firm in your faith through sacrifice will likely look different than mine, it is a reality many of us will face in this post-Christian era that we live. The pandemic brought our current society's rejection of the authority of Christianity, despite the country's founding on Christian ideals, front and center. Our faith was under overt assault and it still is. Our churches were shut down. Our governments ordered us to stay home and refrain from fellowshipping and arrested pastors when they held church services. They required us to cover our faces, made in God's own image, and demanded we mask that very image made to reflect the light of Christ that lives inside us. Social media made mask wearing fashionably noble, while scripture was telling me otherwise.

> "Now the Lord is the Spirit, and where the Spirit of the Lord is, there is freedom. And we all, with *UNVEILED FACES*, beholding the glory of the Lord, are being transformed into the same image from one degree of glory to another."
> —Corinthians 3:17–18

By removing the Spirit of the Lord from the discussion on how to tackle the pandemic, they removed our freedoms. It only took one generation to forget about God after they entered the Promised Land. I wouldn't let it be mine. God was at the center of all the decisions I made during that time. Discernment was the main tool I employed, coupled with the belt of truth. God prompted me to share what I was reading in scripture, like the verse above, with others on social media. This was my way of coming alongside those that were experiencing similar struggles during the mandates. Many disagreed with me but I still pushed forward, knowing instinctually never to doubt the Bible and being encouraged by an influx of messages from some followers on social media that the scripture I was studying and information I was acquiring and sharing was helping others, despite those that lashed out.

At the start of the pandemic in March 2020, were promised thirty days to stop the spread and then the pandemic would be over. That man-made promise was soon forgotten, and those thirty days of lockdown were extended into months. We were promised a shot that was safe and effective and that it would end the pandemic. Yet, vaccinated people got COVID and experienced side effects, and even in some cases death from the shot. Miscarriages and still births were also a tragic side effect.[8] The sanctity of life was left in the dust. Empty promises decimated the Land of the "Free."

Influencers were paid to promote the shots, masking, lockdowns, etc. on social media.[9] All of which became more than just the cool thing to do; it was declared righteous on all of our social media feeds. Never was it clearer that the evil one uses money to promote his agenda, but in the end, we know Who wins and that the Lord always provides if you walk in His ways.

At that time, there was nothing left to do but dive into scripture. God's promises would not be erased from my heart and would be passed down to the next generation; not just through words, but through action. Opening my Bible, I read over and over again that when someone is referenced covering their face in scripture, it is done so out of shame, as Proverbs 30:32 shows:

> "If you have been foolish, exalting yourself, or if you have been devising evil, put your hand on your mouth."
> —Proverbs 30:32

I was not ashamed to opt-out of the COVID-19 shot. And you should never be ashamed to follow your faith, when faced with any controversial circumstance. Look to scripture to be your guide. I was canceled online for my Biblical stance on masks, while the public health officials promoted on every news station, social media channel, and media entity exalted the shots and masks.

Studies from as far back as 2015 have now surfaced that show masks can lead to miscarriage and stillbirths, and do not stop the spread of aerosol viruses.[10] Later, we discovered that Pfizer not only had clinical trial data showing the risks of the shots, but also had a report dated February 28, 2021, that showed in the first ninety days of rollout they knew of 42,086 adverse reactions, 29,914 in women, which included 28 of 32 known pregnancy outcomes resulted in a miscarriage or neonatal death.[11]

Only knowing some of those facts at the time, therefore relying on discernment and scripture to be my guide, I took my God-given role as a pregnant mother, obligated to protect my unborn child, seriously. And I took my role as a Christian, who is supposed to adhere to scripture, seriously. So, I applied for a religious exemption from masking and testing.

I was denied, but I wasn't willing to sacrifice my place in the Kingdom of Heaven. I could not go against my convictions because as James 4:17 states, "whoever knows the right thing to do and fails to do it, for him it is sin." It was worth the persecution on social media, in my profession, and in my personal relationships, and I'd endure it for the Lord again.

I share my story with you, to give an example of using the Faith Filter to wade through a tough situation. No matter how you feel about the handling of COVID, I pray you can see how choosing to answer to God, not society and outside pressures of the day is possible. If I can look to God as the only "like" that matters in situations of big sacrifice, you can too! You will make it through any sacrifice you are called to make. Social media shaming is not the end! You'll never regret following the Word of God in any circumstance. The social media mob attacked me. Not only did I lose my job, but I received death threats, death wishes on my family, and various other vicious attacks thrown my way on my social media feed and private messages. But God gave me the strength to stand firm and push forward.

As a result of my sacrifice to lose my job so as not to compromise my religious beliefs, I experienced cancel culture—which can take on many forms. Cancel culture is experienced by many today, including our youth, and isn't just confined to the deplatforming of public personalities. It also can take on the form of being canceled by your peers through ostracization, harassment, shaming, and bullying on social media–something anyone, no matter their following, can experience. Unfortunately, it is now an addition to the modern struggles of our youth.

Tragically, too many young people have sacrificed their precious lives to suicide because of treatment they've endured online. From having an embarrassing photo or video posted online; to being ridiculed or teased; publicly bullied; or simply feeling like they are not enough compared to what they see online, the world of social media has opened the doors to an entirely new outlet of pressures and persecution for our youth. And for some, it's too much to bear.

Many are even coerced into harming themselves or someone else. The overall rate of suicide in the United States increased in 2021 to 47,646, after declining the two years prior. Males fifteen- to twenty-four-years-old had the largest rate of increase that year.[12] Even harder to quantify are the thousands that have fallen prey to predators, pornography, or sex trafficking via online outlets.

It's likely you have been deeply and psychologically impacted because of the treatment—whether through pressuring, ostracization, harassment, bullying, etc.—you may have received online. But you don't have to carry that alone! Jesus takes up the yoke alongside you. [Matthew 11:30] He can also sympathize with your experience [Hebrews 4:15] because he has been there, too.

Jesus was canceled in the most brutal fashion we've ever seen, by the Pharisees and Sadducees who wanted to take his platform away. Jesus was viscously canceled and rose from the dead three days later. He, too, faced a mob that cried out for his end. Nowadays, the public square is social media, and the mob is powered by keyboards, their cries heard in Tweets of 140 characters or less. Jesus still became the most influential figure in all of history and his truths have withstood the test of time in the most popular book ever. Cancel culture lost and will always lose because "Christ always leads us in triumphal procession." [2 Corinthians 2:14] And when we turn to him in our darkest times we will triumph, too.

I know it may seem like the world is caving in around you when you are in the middle of a tough situation, or public or private harassment and bullying for your faith or any other personal situation, and it's hard to see a way out—especially when you are young. But I am here to speak to you from the other side. The journey is how you work *out* your salvation, not *for* your salvation. You arrive on the other side a stronger, more resilient person, closer to God. Just like someone at the gym works out to make their body stronger, you are inspired by the free gift of salvation to exercise and strengthen your faith to make yourself more like Jesus each day. This is known theologically as the process of sanctification. I remember a day when social media didn't exist. And there will be a day when it or the bullying or harassment you've received on it will no longer plague you and are a thing of the past.

> "For I consider that the sufferings of this present time are not worth comparing with the glory that is to be revealed to us." —Romans 8:18

Look past the screen in your hand and into eternity. Eternity is worth any sacrifice, it's worth any amount of persecution, and it is yours because he paid the perfect sacrifice that you can't and don't have to. Anything you go through online or in this life is fleeting and not comparable to the glory that awaits you with God in heaven.

In his second letter to the church in Corinth, the apostle Paul gives us an exhausted list of everything he's been through (and I'm paraphrasing) from being blinded and shipwrecked, to being lowered in a basket out of a window to escape death, all before his eventual martyrdom. And he ends that message with some choice words given to Paul from God Himself:

> "But he said to me, 'My grace is sufficient for you, for my power is made perfect in weakness.' Therefore, I will boast all the more gladly about my weaknesses, so that Christ's power may rest on me. That is why, for Christ's sake, I delight in weaknesses, in insults, in hardships, in persecutions, in difficulties. For when I am weak, then I am strong."
> —2 Corinthians 12:9–10

You are stronger than your trials, you are stronger than any shaming you've endured online, and you are stronger than the grip that social media has on you, because Christ's power rests on you. He has given you the Armor of God to put on, clothed you with the garments of salvation, and covered you with the robe of righteousness. [Ephesians 6:11, Isaiah 61:10] Further, the possible discipleship relationships that He's provided to help get you through or to glorify Him on the other side of your sacrifice, could bless you beyond what you may realize.

Chapter 9 Devotional

1. List the various trials, tribulations, and sacrifices Jesus had to endure in his life here on earth:

2. As a follower of Christ, do you groan when faced with sacrifices of your own? Name one small sacrifice you complain about:

3. Name one big sacrifice or trial you've faced with difficulty. How did God help you overcome it?

4. Have the sacrifices listed above brought you closer to Christ? If so, how?

5. We know from John 15:20 that a servant is not greater than his master. So, let's look at what Jesus speaks about in that entire passage. Read John 15:18–27 and fill in the blanks from the verse:

- (v. 18) "If the world hates _____ , know that it has hated _____ before it hated you."

- Therefore from John 15:18 we can gather that as followers of Christ, when society shuns you for your beliefs or a stance you take in faith, they are really rejecting _____ .

- (v. 19) "If you were of the _____ , the world would _____ you as its own; but because you are _____ of the world, but I chose you _____ of the world, therefore the world hates you."

6. Look up these supporting passages. Write down what sticks out to you from each:
   - John 3:19
   - Romans 1:21–32
   - 2 Timothy 3:12
   - Psalm 25:19–20
   - Matthew 10:22
   - Amos 5:10
   - Galatians 4:16

7. How do these passages put your heart at ease to know that when someone rejects you, it is because you are standing with Christ? Does it make their rejection of you less personal? Or easier to bear, knowing that no matter the outcome if you stand with or for Jesus that sacrifice will be worth it?

Faith Filter Challenge

8. Read 1 Corinthians 1:18 and fill in the blanks from the verse:

"For the word of the cross is _____ to those that are _____ , but to us who are being saved it is the power of _____."

• What does that mean?

9. We discussed in Chapter 6 how the Beatitudes seem backwards. 1 Corinthians 1:18 shows us that everything about your beliefs as a Christian will seem backwards to the world. How does that reframe your mindset on persecution?

10. Look up Matthew 10:22 again. Does "but the one who endures to the end will be saved," take on greater clarity or importance to you now? How?

11. What is one way you are going against the world now or doing something for your faith that feels unpopular?

12. How can applying the Faith Filter to that situation after doing this devotional adjust your outlook on it?

13. Let's end this study by revisiting words of encouragement from the Apostle Paul:

"But he said to me, 'My grace is sufficient for you, for my power is made perfect in weakness.' Therefore, I will boast all the more gladly about my weaknesses, so that Christ's power may rest on me. That is why, for Christ's sake, I delight in weaknesses, in insults, in hardships, in persecutions, in difficulties. For when I am weak, then I am strong."
—2 Corinthians 12:9–10

Prayer

Dear Lord,

Thank You for giving me strength, even in my weakest moments. Thank You for providing me faith when I am walking through sacrifice. Thank You for your grace. May Christ's power rest on me. Help me to find joy in taking up my cross daily. This road can be weary and I am broken, tired, and in need of a heart check often. Remind me that we are not of this world, therefore the world will hate us. But blessed are the persecuted, for theirs is the kingdom of heaven. Thank You for providing me with everything I need in scripture. Point me back to Your Word more often for encouragement, as I walk by faith, regardless of what the world says.

Amen.

Chapter 10

Discipleship

The spotless lambs that were nurtured in the ceremonious birthing caves—that some scholars believe Jesus was born in—were cared for specifically by Levitical Shepherds. They were of the bloodline of the Tribe of Levi, a chosen priesthood, trained to take care of the special flocks of sacrificial lambs. Today, we are the Lord's shepherds called to take care of each other, help those in need, and share the Good News of Jesus Christ with all whom we can.

> "But you are a chosen people, a royal priesthood, a holy nation, a people belonging to God, that you may declare the praises of him who called you out of darkness into his wonderful light." –1 Peter 2:9

The first people to see the light of the angels that God sent to announce the birth of His Son were shepherds. This is no coincidence. It is *also* no coincidence that shepherds were considered outcasts at that time, just as the Son's followers would come to be known at various points in history. On par with prostitutes (Rahab) and tax collectors (Matthew), shepherds (David) were shunned by townspeople as dirty, vile, and unclean workers who handled animals all day. Yet, they were the chosen messengers to deliver the good news of the birth of Jesus Christ.

You'll notice God did not choose the Pharisees—Bethlehem's elite or most popular people with the largest audience—to share this news. Instead, He chose shepherds, outcasts, the least popular to share His message. That is us. That is you. You don't have to have a large contingent of followers to shepherd others. Your soul influence is strongest on the people around you. Your message is most likely received by those not yearning for the material things of this world, but the unseen gifts brought by the Ultimate Influencer.

Shepherds are tasked with the job of nurturing and taking care of their flock, leading them back when they are led astray and keeping them on path when they are walking in the right direction. Jesus declares himself to be our Good Shepherd [John 10:11] and many refer to the pastors of their own churches as shepherds of their congregation.

King David, whose sin we learned came from promiscuity and idleness, was a shepherd who honed his skills in the field. Those skills of defending his flock from lions and bears led him to slay the giant. He was a shepherd whose love for God made him fit to become a king and earn the title of the Shepherd King of Israel. He's also the very man who was a descendant of the Good Shepherd. And the Good Shepherd himself tasked us with being shepherds, or disciples, not just sharing the Good News but showing others what following the Father, Son, and Holy Spirit looks like and teaching them to stay on path. [Matthew 28:19–20]

Jesus gave that Great Commission to his twelve closest followers, delivering it to them forty days after his resurrection, just before he ascended into heaven. Do you think the disciples were very popular guys at that point in time? At a time when they were going around telling people their former teacher had come back from the dead and was popping up around the region, appearing to those that needed his miracles? I bet many believed they sounded crazy! Yet,

God chose them to be the ones to go forth and share Jesus's story so that we and the whole world would know about him today. They went on to influence countless souls. And we are called to do so as well. The Great Commission applies to us all, regardless of the number of followers next to our name on our social media profile.

"Go therefore and make disciples of all nations, baptizing them in the name of the Father and of the Son and of the Holy Spirit, teaching them to observe all that I have commanded you. And behold, I am with you always, to the end of the age."
—Matthew 28:19–20

In 2019, I walked out of the sanctuary after church service and was approached by a woman asking me to be in a small group bible study led by her and her husband. "Yes," came out of my mouth before I even knew what I was saying. The Holy Spirit prompted me to agree, even though my husband and I had never been in a small group bible study and were only attending that church periodically, as our work schedules would allow. Sunday is a popular day for golf, and we were both in the thick of our golf careers. I'll let you connect the dots on what our priorities were at the time.

After we started attending the weekly study, we quickly became friends with the other couples of various ages and walks of life. The woman who initially asked me to attend was assigned as my "Faith Friend" by the women's ministry at the church and invited me to come to coffee with her once per week to pray and do a quick devotional. Soon thereafter, we no longer had to put our coffee dates on the schedule—we were naturally friends and organically made time for one another.

Her discipleship changed my life. The shepherding she and her husband did for our family was a living example of a fruitful walk with the Lord, and I was inspired to share the fruit of that walk with others. In 2020, at the height of my career, I wrote this book in some of those coffee shops where we began our discipleship together. That same year, the Lord put the idea of Driving Disciples, a bible study and golf camp, on our hearts—a mission my husband and I could have never carried through without both our mentors' time and support.

As only the Lord would have it, in the wake of my firing, she and another wonderful sister in Christ met me at that same local coffee shop. They both prayed over me in one of my darkest points. All those times we had joyfully prayed together at coffee shops, dove into the Word together, and just lived life together with her pointing to Jesus as the center of it all had led to this moment. Their support not only equipped me for the storm but gave me the tools to guide me through it and see hope on the other side. It gave me hope and a clear mission.

I had to do the same for others. I, too, had to be a disciple.

If you follow me on social media, you wouldn't know this woman, but her impact is imbued in all my efforts, although not directly. None of my content is her direct opinion or close work. But her friendship and spiritual guidance have influenced me far beyond the content on my channels. Being a disciple and soul influencer isn't a measurable job. It's likely not one outwardly displayed on social media. But it is intentional, it is fruitful, and it is a true marker of one in Christ.

> "Just as I have loved you, you also should love one another.
> By this everyone will know that you are my disciples,
> if you have love for one another."
> —John 13:34–35

I was a Christian and loved God with all my heart, but my friend's discipleship drew me closer to God, in a pivotal time in my life. Both because of what soon came with my public career struggle, but also as I entered into motherhood, and my husband and I were searching for a closer relationship with God to build our family's foundation on. Discipleship is the key to it all. It's what opens the door in your own life, so you can keep the doors open for others.

During COVID, doors were shut. Many churches willingly shut their doors per the government's orders. These regulations came at a time when more than 50 percent of kids growing up in the church were leaving as an adult.[13] For many who left the church, it was merely something you did on special holidays and the occasional Sunday. But your communal walk is so much more than that.

Social media can help to make our collective worship a daily habit, as we share with each other theological ideas that inspire us, pass along a clip from a sermon that moves us, invite someone to an event another church is promoting on their social media page, etc. Discipleship can be facilitated through our devices, as a way for us to easily remind each other daily of the Good News.

"But exhort one another every day, as long as it is called 'today.'"
—Hebrews 3:13

That said, fellowship, friendship, and face-to-face living life together is essential. It always has been the key ingredient of our human makeup, but it's at the top of the list now in this digital age. As we learn to consume, operate, and approach social media from a biblical worldview, we also must work hard to move beyond social media to have an in-person impact. This digital age makes it harder and scarier to step away from our screens, but periodically taking a break is essential for discipleship.

In-person discipleship is the only way we can help reduce the suicide rate.

It's the only way we can help lower the amount of people turning away from God into adulthood.

It's the only way we can prevent our girls from sharing provocative photos online and boys from falling prey to porn.

The only way is to show each other Jesus; to encourage each other in Christ. While the world pushes against Him, it is essential to feel in community with one another. Social media can connect and build this community, but that is just the start. Let it be the catalyst to us realizing we need to limit time on our phones and get back to walking in faith together—face-to-face. Developing a relationship with Christ gives a person the tools to rise above the anxieties of social media and tackle hardship, which in turn can inspire them to go out and influence someone else in a positive way by spreading God's Word.

If I can make this book a reality and my husband and I can rely on our faith to push us to start a ministry in the middle of job loss, new babies, and a world of uncertainty, there's no doubt that all things are possible with God. [Matthew 19:26] The last line of the Great Commission calling us to be disciples, the very last thing Jesus says before ascending into heaven is, "behold, I am with you always, till the end of the age." [Matthew 28:19]

He is with us through everything. Even if you don't know how, He will equip you to be a disciple. Once you've experienced and realized the fullness of His grace, gifts, and comfort, you can't help but share that with others. As a shepherd, you nurture that love of Christ in others, pointing them back to Him in everything they do, in every circumstance. You are a soul influencer, a disciple, a chosen son or daughter of God and the joy of the Lord is your strength. [Nehemiah 8:10]

Work up the strength to join a small group and find a church family. Humble yourself to be open to someone discipling you and before you know it, you'll become an active disciple yourself.

Chapter 10 Devotional

1. Titus 2 is a classic Biblical example of what good shepherds
   in the Christian community look like. Let's break down what
   the Bible says we should look for or emulate if we are teaching sound doctrine to each other. Read each verse indicated
   below and list out the attributes given in scripture.

   (Titus 2:2) Older men are to be:
   1.)   4.)
   2.)   5.)
   3.)   6.)

   (v. 3) Older women are to be:
   1.)   3.)
   2.)   4.)

   (v. 4–5) Therefore older women are to teach the younger
   women to:
   1.)   4.)
   2.)   5.)
   3.)   6.)

   (v. 6) Likewise urge the younger men to be:

   _____

2. Which category do you fall under? Do you embody any of
   those characteristics?

3. Do you have someone that is discipling you? If so, do they embody any of the characteristics from Titus 2:2–6?

4. If you find yourself to be a mentor, do you possess any of the characteristics from Titus 2:2–3? Are there any characteristics you'd like to improve on? How do you plan to do so?

5. Read Titus 2:12. It says that as disciples God is "training us to renounce _____ & _____ passions, and to live _____-_____ , upright, and _____ lives in the present age."

   • Are there any areas in your social media activity that you still need to work on exercising self-control?

   • Have you made improvements in this area since you started reading this book and doing the devotionals?

SOUL INFLUENCE CHALLENGE

6. Write down someone who you'd like to mentor you, or someone you'd like to be a mentor to right now:

7. What steps are you going to take this week to become their "faith friend"?

8. If you connect with them on social media, how can you take it a step further and nurture your relationship in a face-to-face setting?

Prayer

Dear Lord,

Thank You for putting people in my life that impact my faith journey. Help me to also be a disciple to others. Equip me with the tools to have an eternal influence through purity and self-control. Reveal to me someone who can be a faith friend to me. Likewise, reveal to me who I can be a faith friend to, as well. Help me to be a grateful companion to someone who is pouring into me. Let me pray for my current mentor and future mentors. That they may be encouraged and lifted up in their fellowship, knowing that they are adorning the Bride of Christ and beautifying his church. Thank You for the chance to learn from them and, in turn, drive others to be disciples for Your Kingdom.

Amen.

Chapter 11

Rest

This book may feel like a call to do more: to study your Bible more often, to share the gospel more, to sharpen your Faith Filter and hone your discernment, to set up more boundaries for yourself on social media. But what God is really calling us to do, is to do less. Consume less of the world. Have your heart broken less by the sin you constantly scroll through. Care less about the big stuff. Rest more in the little things. Recognize the fast-paced world technology has brought us and make an effort to slow down.

These days, we are more likely to know of all the bad happening in the world as a whole rather than the struggles of the neighborhoods in which we live. We are fed headlines from China, the Middle East, and the rest of the world, but we aren't privy to the hardships of our neighbor two houses down or the ways we can get involved at church. We should be less emotionally charged about the shortcomings of Washington, D.C., and more about who we are voting into our local school board or the needs of our family or community.

Despite being "connected" more than ever, we are less plugged in than ever before. Fewer of us are serving in our communities, Lions Clubs, Rotary Clubs, or on our church boards. You'll become aware of these opportunities to plug back into your community when you become intentional about putting your phone down for a few minutes in the hallway at church to look at the service bulletin board or chat with your neighbor two houses down.

Strike up a conversation, learn about their needs, take action by partnering up with your faith friends to help lighten that neighbor's load. My current women's small group has a group text, where, oftentimes, we share our prayer requests that involve our needs or needs of others in our lives. This dialogue has led to someone's spiritual or emotional needs being tended to more times that I can count. Neighbors who have no one to help them have had their cats fed while they were away; sick patients have been visited in the hospital; struggling relationships are prayed for; students have been offered internship opportunities. All because we slowed down for a few minutes and communicated with one another in our small group.

Prior to the internet, people consumed the news via their local newspaper; talked in their neighborhood churches, coffee shops, and hair salons; and then sat down once per night for thirty minutes or less to receive the headlines from their favorite national anchor. What if you did the same? Instead of scrolling through the world news when you wait in line for your bagel, tuck your phone away and talk to the person next to you. Instead of watching church on YouTube, go to church early and stay after the sermon to congregate with your fellow church goers. (Maybe you'll meet the mentor that will change your life!) Rather than consuming social media periodically all day long, give yourself a small slice of time each day to consume what you need to, and then put your phone down. Hold yourself to the One-One-One Rule. Spend the rest of your spare time studying the Word, reading books, communicating with loved ones, being present for your family, finally trying that new hobby or project you've been eyeing on Instagram, and interacting with your neighbors.

Social media is a product, but in many ways we ourselves have become the product. Our information and interests are being bought and sold to company advertisers as you blissfully scroll on your device. Facebook, Instagram, and Twitter make $44 billion per year selling *your* data.[14] They make all that money in exchange for you to use the platforms for free, all while they harvest and store your data without you even thinking about it. We might not feel like we have control of that harsh consumer-driven reality, but what you do have control over is your consumption habits.

A not-so-secret industry secret is that content creators and platforms are competing for your time. Their number one job is to get you to stay on their pages as long as possible. The longer you stay there, the more data they can collect to sell, the more advertisements they can show you, etc. Social media feeds you as much content as it can, so when you are done with one story, they can keep you on their platform with the next. They are purposefully trying to get you to spend your time with them, for better or worse. Part of being a responsible consumer is knowing what your threshold is. How much can you consume before you reach your end point? Chances are most of us are going well beyond our max. By caring less for what you are seeing on these platforms, it allows you to loosen the pull they have on you.

Is the device in your pocket weighing you down? Then leave it in the other room for a bit. Ask God to give you the strength to break your addiction to it. Our phones don't control us. Jesus has set us free. Care less about that little black device. Care more about Him. And when you must pick it back up, use the tools He has given us. Use the Faith Filter, put on the Armor of God, consume content that has an eternal influence on you instead of a social influence. Surrender your heart, your mind, and your consumption habits to Jesus. While the things we see on social media put the weight of the globe on our shoulders, Jesus takes the other yoke upon his back for us. [Matthew 11:30]

"They promise them freedom, but they themselves are slaves of
corruption, since people are enslaved to whatever defeats them."
—2 Peter 2:19 CSB

Social media cannot defeat you when you care about God more than anything else. All other things will slowly lose their grip on you. However, you can't conquer your device if you are a slave to it and unable to take time away from it. Since our phones are always right there with us, we never seem to get a break. We are constantly plugged into work, the world, and the news, perpetually beating ourselves up for not limiting more of our time in those areas. Switch up your strategy. Redirect your rest. Instead of "taking a break" on your device, rest in the Lord.

Only nine percent of Americans attend church weekly,[15] which means 91 percent of us are not even giving ourselves the chance to rest on the Lord's Day by allowing our souls to worship, as we are commanded to do. And if you do fall into that nine percent of church-goers, what do you do for the rest of the day when you aren't in church? Are you, admittedly like me, making yourself busy? Catching up on emails you may have missed over the weekend? Thinking about what you need to do for the week ahead? Scrolling through social media in an effort to zone out and "take a break"? Is that really rest as the Lord commands?

Rest is freedom from the guilt of sin or the anxieties that plague us. How can you achieve that rest if you are still scrolling online?! Only in Christ can we be truly at rest. Only through his blood are our sins forgiven. Accepting the gift of grace is the only way we can rest from our affliction.

"Come to me, all who labor and are heavy laden, and I will give you
rest. Take my yoke upon you, and learn from me, for I am gentle and
lowly in heart, and you will find rest for your souls."
—Matthew 11:28 & 29

When we dove into "surrender" in Chapter 8, Hebrews 4 showed us that we have a High Priest that *can* sympathize with our weakness. He's been here in flesh; he knows we need this rest. Our salvation depends on it.

"Therefore, since the promise of entering his rest still stands, let us be careful that none of you be found to have fallen short of it."
—Hebrews 4:1

"It still remains that some will enter that rest, and those who formerly had the gospel preached to them did not go in, because of their disobedience."
—Hebrews 4:6

When God gave Moses the Ten Commandments, He emphasized in the fourth commandment that we are to honor the Sabbath Day. Many of the other commandments are a simple statement, but God takes special care to describe this commandment as a day of rest where we "shall not do any work" because "the Lord blessed the Sabbath day and made it holy." [Exodus 20:10–11] The New Testament reiterates that we must rest on the seventh day.

"There remains, then, a Sabbath-rest for the people of God;
for anyone who enters God's rest also rests from
his own work, just as God did from his.
Let us, therefore, make every effort to enter that rest, so that no one
will fall by following their example of disobedience."
—Hebrews 4:9–11

In the busy times we live in, do we really, truly rest? Why do we blow it off? Is it because we don't know how to rest anymore? Have we been trained by our devices to keep ourselves busy?

Many of us think "zoning out" out on our devices counts as rest. But that is really not rest. We need to learn the real meaning of rest, according to scripture. First Hebrews 4:11 emphasizes that we must enter rest so that we don't fall into disobedience by breaking the fourth commandment. The fourth commandment, even in New Testament times, is important for us to follow because it turns our heart toward God for at least one day per week.

> "For the word of God is living and active, sharper than any two-edged sword, piercing to the division of soul and of spirit, of joints and of marrow, and discerning the thoughts and intentions of the heart. And no creature is hidden from his sight, but all are naked and exposed to the eyes of him to whom we must give account. Since then we have a great high priest who has passed through the heavens, Jesus, the Son of God, let us hold fast our confession. For we do not have a high priest who is unable to sympathize with our weaknesses, but one who in every respect has been tempted as we are, yet without sin."
> —Hebrews 4:12–15

Next, Hebrews 4:12 goes on to define rest by explaining, "the word of God is living and active, sharper than any two-edged sword." This is inferring that we are to rest in God's Word! We are to rest by turning our hearts to God through the reading of God's Word.

Maybe you are thinking to yourself, *reading the Bible sounds like work. That doesn't sound like rest to me.* Traditionally, the Sabbath Day was meant to set aside uninterrupted time to worship God, fellowship, and rest from all other work and obligations so we could take our mind off the worries of this world and rest by turning our attention to God, who can ease our hearts. Worship and focusing on God has always traditionally involved diving into His Word, both collectively as a church body during Sunday service and individually in our private, peaceful study that same day.

The passage goes on to describe God's Word as able to discern the thoughts and intentions of the heart [Hebrews 4:12b]. If we take time to reflect on our praises, trials, and worries, we can then take those to God in prayer. At the same time we go to prayer, we can also confess our shortcomings. Because Hebrews 4:13 goes on to tell us that nothing "is hidden from His sight." He knows everything we do, everything that crosses our minds, everything we consume, so therefore we must take everything to "him to whom we must give an account." [Hebrews 4:14]

In summary, Hebrews 4 provides the formula for rest: read, reveal, reflect, and finally, receive. By *reading* God's Word, it *reveals* to us our shortcomings as we evaluate ourselves in comparison with scripture and allows space to *reflect* on how we can improve in our Christian walk and therefore confess to the Lord where we need to.

When you confess your sins, you are starting a true, soul-influencing dialogue with Christ. That's when the passage from Hebrews 4:15 comes in, reminding us that we have a high priest who can sympathize with our weaknesses. He knows and cares about your confession. He sympathizes with you in that moment of revealing your weaknesses to Him. Love flows forth from the Savior when you lay it all at the altar.

> "Let us then with confidence draw near to the throne of grace, that we may receive mercy and find grace."
> —Hebrews 4:16

After reflection and confession, then we can finally soak in the last part of the rest formula: receive. *Receiving* mercy and grace from the Lord, that is *rest*. Letting it all go, laying it all out there, getting it off your chest, knowing that it will be received and forgiven by the Savior who is gentle and lowly at heart. This is freedom from whatever is defeating you, even if just for the day or those short moments of confession and relationship with Christ. When you are set free from sin and guilt, and receive His mercy and grace, then you can rest.

Rest. That's what we are commanded to do and how your cup is filled. That's how your soul is influenced. That is how you will come to truly realize the only "like" that matters is God's.

Chapter 11 Devotional

1. Following up from the Chapter 10 devotional, who did you attempt to foster a "faith friend" relationship with? How did it go? What steps can you take to continue that soul influence this week?

2. How do you currently "rest"?

3. Would you consider zoning out on your device "rest"? Or do you need to redirect your rest strategy after reading this final chapter?

4. Do you honor the Sabbath? On that day, do you rest in the Lord and foster that relationship with Him in the reading of His Word, meditation, reflection, confession?

5. What is keeping you from that time in relationship with Him? Is it your device?

6. Let's practice the formula from Hebrews 4.

   • Read Hebrews 4:1–16. What did that reveal to you about your own thoughts or actions?

   • Reflect to God about how you'd like help to improve yourself in those areas and confess your shortcomings with a short prayer:

   • Rest by receiving His mercy and grace, setting yourself free from those things. How do you feel?

SOUL INFLUENCE CHALLENGE

7. Open your calendar and block out time to attend church this Sunday.
   - Also indicate on your calendar a fifteen-minute block of time that day for private bible reading and the Hebrews 4 rest formula.

8. Who is someone you see on occasion in your neighborhood, grocery store, school, etc., that you have never struck up an in-depth conversation with? This week, make a point to say hello to them. Ask them about what is going on in their life right now and how you can pray for them.

   - Their Prayer Request:

   - Pray all week for them and ask them about it next time you see them.

Prayer

Dear Lord,

Please give me the strength to truly rest. Help me to intentionally allow myself the time and space to dive into the Word with you. Show me how to rest in our relationship, containing dialogue and confession. Help me to feel true freedom from my shortfallings. Help me to learn how to receive your mercy and grace. Influence my soul today. Bring me back to You each Sabbath. Allow that to carry over into my relationships with others, so that I can help others realize your "like" is the only one that matters.

Amen.

Afterword

We are all on a journey in our relationship with Christ, not only experiencing highs and lows, but also times where we are closer to Him or farther away. But just like a good friend, when you come back together after time apart, there are no hard feelings. Instead grace, mercy, and love are abundant, and it feels like hardly any time has passed when you finally do meet again.

I admit I wrote Chapter 11 on rest during a very busy season in my life. This was a sobering one to write. My current shortcomings in my walk with the Lord were staring me right in the face as I typed. I felt hypocritical at times. But it did allot me the time and reflection to remind myself that I, too, needed to rest. Rest in Him. Rest in freedom from my fast-paced projects, to reflect, confess, and build myself into a better mom, wife, daughter, friend, and person, through time with Him. That reflection time was needed!

So just know, even the person who wrote that last chapter needs a reminder just as much as anyone. We all go through our busy seasons, our slow seasons, our seasons close to Him and far away. Even though we fade in and out, He is always there. His whispers kept me going through it all, telling me it was "okay" and "rest was coming soon." He kept encouraging me, and it was the dialogue that I needed in this particular season.

Rest is around the corner. I know that as I type this to you because of that relationship I built with Him. The building blocks of a deeper relationship, assembled in the depths of walking *sola fide*–Latin for by faith alone. Those times brought me the deepest conversations with the Lord I've ever had. And also gave me the confidence to know He gave us the authority to say, "Satan be bound!"

I look forward to more deep dialogue with the Lord to come. In a slower time. In a more restful, far-less tumultuous time.

Rest comes in ebbs and flows in this life. And we can all look forward to rest beyond our wildest dreams in eternity.

God Bless.

—Teryn

Biblical Social Media Tools Appendix

Faith Filter: The lens through which you take in every piece of content or information that you come across and is how you see the world. Do you embrace a piece of content as biblically true, dismiss it as biblically inaccurate, or investigate it because you are unsure of how it measures up to scripture? It can also influence your behaviors and attitude and can move you to glorify God in most every area of your life.

- Apply the Faith Filter to social media and all areas of your life.

Social Media as a Tool: Remove social media as an idol in your life and instead see it as a place where you use the "Faith Filter" to navigate at all times.

- View social media as a *tool* to bolster your Christian walk and as an *enhancement* to your worship and study of God—not a replacement to bypass the work we all have to put into our faith journey.
- Social media can help to make our collective worship a daily habit, as we share with each other theological ideas that inspire us, pass along a clip from a sermon that moves us, invite someone to an event another church is promoting on their social media page, etc.
- Do not view it as a *replacement* for your time reading the Bible or your in-person fellowship because you

consume photos of verses on Instagram instead, or joined a Facebook chat instead of a bible study group, or watch sermons online.

One-One-One Challenge: One hour per day, one day per week, one week per year, take a break from your phone. [Adapted from Andy Crouch of *The Tech Wise Family*]
- Perform the One-One-One Challenge as a way to be more present and intentional with your relationship with God and others and as a way to enhance your time on social media when you do return from each break.

Soul Influence: The influence each of us has on people's *souls*, particularly those around us—our friends, family, and loved ones. You have influence on their eternal standing with our Creator, their views on themselves as children of God, and their place in the Kingdom.
- Recognize you are a soul influencer, regardless of the size of your social media platform.

Gratitude: (verb) – With God as your guiding light, intentionally adjust your attitude and heart posture by picking up your Bible and reminding yourself and your family daily of God's grace. When His "like" is all we truly need, God in His fullness of grace, glory and goodness is what motivates us to *practice* gratitude
- Practice gratitude by intentionally adjusting your outlook and removing comparison from your social media roadblocks.

The Ultimate Influencer: Jesus was the original influencer. He is the first and the last—the No. 1 influencer we should look to. [Revelation 22:13] Jesus has influenced billions of people in the two thousand years since his death. No other person even comes close. Jesus invented the "follow" button and instructs us to follow him more than twenty times in the Gospels.

- Look to Jesus as your model and follow him as the Ultimate Influencer.

Time Tracking Challenge: Use your phone's Settings to track your time on social media vs. reading the Bible.
- Reference the Chapter 6 devotional to see how you can set a time limit on social media or other apps and how to gain insights into your time spent per day online.

Discernment: The ability to decipher the world around you with spiritual guidance from The Holy Spirit, who will equip you with the tools you need to continue using social media, by navigating it from a place of freedom as a new person in Christ.
- Look at the Armor of God to acquire those tools and cultivate your discernment online.

Memory Verse Screen Saver: Using your favorite Bible App, screenshot a verse or series of verses you'd like to memorize for the week. Set it as your screen saver and challenge yourself to memorize it. Read it *before* opening up social media, messages, or email. Then cut your time on those outlets short to go back to working on your memory verse again afterward. Let it sink in and teach yourself of various scriptures diligently, "when you sit in your house, and when you walk by the way, and when you lie down, and when you rise." [Deuteronomy 6:7]
- Create a Memory Verse Screen Saver to help you to continue to surrender your device to the Lord.

Faith Friend: A mentor to you or someone you are mentoring in a discipleship relationship, that may begin by intentionally setting aside time to regularly meet to pray, do a quick devotional with, and experience life-on-life shepherding.
- Find or develop an in-person "Faith Friend" relationship, that can be enhanced through your use of social media, as a tool to easily remind each other often of the Good News.

Rest: Rest in God's Word, using the Hebrews 4 formula from Chapter 11, for rest: read, reveal, reflect, and receive, and slowly break the habit of zoning out on your device to "rest."

- By *reading* God's Word, it *reveals* to us our shortcomings as we evaluate ourselves in comparison with scripture and allows space to *reflect* on how we can improve in our Christian walk and therefore confess to the Lord where we need to. *Receive* mercy and grace from the Lord to set yourself free from sin and guilt, so that you can rest.

Acknowledgments

Thank you to my husband, who has never questioned God's plan and has always pushed us forward walking by faith, not sight. Thank you to our children who continue to bless us beyond belief and showed me that life is so much more than a career. To my parents, who have always been my biggest supporters and rock. And to our friends, family, and church family who have stuck by our side through this crazy journey, encouraging us when we needed it most and offering suggestions while looking over this manuscript.

God has been in every bit of it all and we wouldn't have it any other way.

And finally, thank you to all of my supporters, whether you've been here since the beginning of my career or have come on board somewhere along the way. Your support and encouragement helps to keep me going.

About the Author

Wife, mom, author, film director, and show host, Teryn Gregson is the co-founder of Driving Disciples—a ministry that is golf inspired by the gospel—which focuses on curriculum and combined youth Bible study and golf camps. Teryn now directs her efforts to her various mission projects including, *Faithful Freedom with Teryn Gregson: Presented by We The Patriots USA,* which is broadcasted nationwide, and is the director and producer of the award-winning documentary *Shot Dead.* Additionally, she creates educational clean-living resources and religious exemption guides on TerynGregson.com. All of this, a stark turn from her more than a decade in sports journalism. Formerly a broadcaster for CBS Sports, Fox Sports Midwest, the St. Louis Cardinals, and finally the PGA TOUR, before being fired for religious discrimination during the pandemic in November 2021. Teryn, her husband Mitchell, and their small children now live in their hometown of Waterloo, IL, where they are focused on their family and homestead.

Endnotes

1 C.D. Gross, "'Jealous' in the Old Testament: The Hebrew Word Qana' and Related Words," *The Bible Translator*, April 1997, https://journals.sagepub.com/doi/abs/10.1177/026009439704800205?journalCode=tbtd

2 Elizabeth Elliot, *Keep a Quiet Heart* (Grand Rapids: Revell, 1995), 58–59.

3 John MacArthur, *James: Guidelines For a Happy Christian Life* (Nashville: Nelson Books, 2007), 16.

4 Christie Allen, "10-Year BYU Study Shows Elevated Suicide Risk From Excess Social Media Time For Young Teen Girls," *BYU News*, February 3, 2021, https://news.byu.edu/intellect/10-year-byu-study-shows-elevated-suicide-risk-from-excess-social-media-time-for-young-teen-girls

5 Angie Smith, *Matchless: The Life and Love of Jesus* (Nashville: Lifeway Press, 2020), 145.

6 Jaco Booyens Ministries, accessed July 18, 2023, https://jacobooyensministries.org/.

7 Jaco Booyens, "Sex Trafficking: REAL Reason Media Is Trying to Push It Out of the Headlines," interview by Teryn Gregson, Faithful Freedom with Teryn Gregson, presented by We The Patriots USA, July 19, 2021, 16:27, https://teryngregson.com/resources/f/sex-trafficking-interview-with-jaco-booyens-ep-101.

8 "Receipt of mRNA COVID-19 Vaccines and Risk of Spontaneous Abortion," *New England Journal of Medicine*, September 8, 2021, https://www.nejm.org/doi/full/10.1056/nejmc2113891

9 "U.S. Department of Health and Human Services Launches Nationwide Network of Trusted Voices to Encourage Vaccination in Next Phase of COVID-19 Public Education Campaign," HHS.gov, April 1, 2021, https://web.archive.org/web/20210401225102/https://www.hhs.gov/about/news/2021/04/01/hhs-launches-nationwide-network-trusted-voices-encourage-vaccination-next-phase-covid-19-public-education-campaign.html

10 P.S.Y. Tong, Kale, A.S., Ng, K. et al., "Respiratory consequences of N95-type Mask usage in pregnant healthcare workers—a controlled clinical study," *Antimicrob Resist Infect Control* 4, 48 (2015). https://doi.org/10.1186/s13756-015-0086-z.

11 Pfizer, "5.3.6 Cumulative Analysis of Post-Authorization Adverse Event Reports of PF-07302048 (BNT162B2)," Received Through 28-Feb-2021: 7, 12, https://phmpt.org/wp-content/uploads/2021/11/5.3.6-post-marketing-experience.pdf.

12 CDC, National Center for Health Statistics, Office of Communications, "Suicide Increases in 2021 After Two Years of Decline," September 30, 2022, https://www.cdc.gov/nchs/pressroom/nchs_press_releases/2022/20220930.htm

13 Jeffrey M. Jones, "In U.S., Childhood Churchgoing Habits Fade in Adulthood," Gallup, December 21, 2022, https://news.gallup.com/poll/467354/childhood-churchgoing-habits-fade-adulthood.aspx?utm_source=alert&utm_medium=email&utm_content=morelink&utm_campaign=syndication

14 Kari Paul, "Americans' Data Is Worth Billions – And Soon You Might Be Able to Get a Cut of It," MarketWatch, October 9, 2018, https://www.marketwatch.com/story/americans-data-is-worth-billions-and-you-soon-might-be-able-to-get-a-cut-of-it-2018-10-09

15 Jeffrey M. Jones, "In U.S., Childhood Churchgoing Habits Fade in Adulthood," Gallup, December 21, 2022, https://news.gallup.com/poll/467354/childhood-churchgoing-habits-fade-adulthood.aspx?utm_source=alert&utm_medium=email&utm_content=morelink&utm_campaign=syndication

Index

Notes